I0413800

Invoking Hitler

B.M. Williams

This is not a work of fiction. Names, characters, places, and incidents are documented. Any resemblance to actual events, locales, organizations, or persons, living or dead, are entirely on purpose and is the intent of the author.

Book Title: Invoking Hitler by B.M. Williams Copyright 2017

ISBN-13: 978-1543057164
ISBN-10: 1543057160

First Printing: February 2017
Printed in the USA

Dedicated to M.T.

Thanks for all the Fish

Table of Contents

Introduction

Since the 1940s when one mentioned "Hitler" or "Nazi", it brought a sense of sadness, anger, patriotism, or historical recollection. Although used in the based sparingly, it has become a staple in American language to invoke either term for an individual they do not agree with. This is not a party issue, as both Republicans and Democrats have widely used the term not only for political opponents, but for international figure heads as well. Those terms immediately invoke a knee-jerk reaction of dislike, anger, and protentional fear. While initially it was used in isolated instances, now it seems that many willingly and without thought will vocally make comparisons with little to no historical references.

The problem with name calling, and especially using terms that are meant to inflict pain is that over time they lose their meaning. World War II was over 70 years ago, many living where not directly impacted by the events of the Nazi party, or Hitler himself. Yes, students learn about the war in school, but it's not the same as those who were directly impacted by Nazi Germany's actions. Citizens of the United States are even distanced further by the fact that the war did not actively occur on their soil. Yes, Pearl Harbor was directed at the United States, but at that time Hawaii was not a state, but a territory. For those living in Germany, there are daily reminders of the war, from memorials, to actual concentration camps.

Leaders in the past have been compared, and leaders in the future will likely as well. Most of the time it is simply name calling, rhetoric to poison voters against your opponent, however recently there has been a change. It is no longer simple name calling, but trying to compare President Donald Trump's actions with those of Adolf Hitler. In the past, history shows invoking Hitler's name was overblown and purely used degrading manner. Now, however, the comparisons are not just to degrade, but to warn, to throw the flag up before it gets too far.

Although this book is focused primarily on the current leadership, a history of smearing one's name by comparing them to Hitler is not a new phenomenon. Starting while Adolf Hitler was still alive, leaders in the United States were likened to him but both external and internal commentators. While a broad study of past utterances is included, it is likely not complete, and there may be presidents, and others who have been compared that are not included in this.

The United States has not seen a leader or followers that resembled Adolf Hitler and the Nazi party until now. The events and leader of the present need to be examined with the historical light of the 1930s and 1940s. There are many that treat this as hot air, just using it to inflict instant outrage. What this book strives to show is that it is not hyperbole, but something that everyone should be considerate of. If nothing else, this book should be a cautionary tale of how after decades of screaming wolf, the wolf has now landed the most prominent position in the United States government. One, that with a stroke of a pen can change and affect millions of lives, be it negatively or positively.

Part One: Rhetoric

But he's still alive...now he's not

When Hitler began to gain power before to 1932, few countries took notice. Many were still deeply entrenched in the Great Depression, and a new mover in Germany was not that much of a worry. Especially since after 1919, the belief was that Germany would not remilitarize. There was also a general sense of isolationism in hopes of regaining some political, economic, and military strength.

There were those who after meeting him in the early 1920s that were impressed with his charisma and ability to capture people's attention. In fact, two individuals, Truman Smith, a junior military attache said of Hitler after meeting him that, "This is a marvelous demagogue who can really inspire loyalty." Karl von Wiegand, the first American journalist to converse with Hitler said that he was "struck by Hitler's oratorical skills and his ability to whip people into a frenzy." Neither of them saw the darkness. Other than that many did not actively concern themselves with him.

In 1923 Hitler lead the Nazi Party in an attempted coup of the government, known as the Beer Hall Putsch. On November 8-9 1923 the Nazi Party descended on Munich with 2000 men marching through the streets. At the end, 16 Nazi's and 4 policemen were killed.[1] It wasn't until the 10th of November that Hitler was arrested and jailed on charges of treason.

---

[1] "Beer Hall Putsch" US Holocaust Museum. Full article can be found: http://bit.ly/2kHHEmu

While in jail, Hitler not only wrote his manifesto, Mein Kompf, but also realized that the only way to gain power is to do it through legal channels, such as being appointed positions or being elected into them. After being released in 1924 after only having served 9 months, Hitler began to gain support. Although he was the leader of the Nazi Party, Hitler laid low until 1932 when with the election, the Nazi Party became the largest elected party. As Hitler was the leader, they appointed him Chancellor in January 1933. After that, it was a marked and thorough change of policies and ideology that lead to not only the Second World War but the death of millions at the hands of a ruthless dictator.

When leaders of other countries began to realize the power that Hitler commanded and the ideology that he believed in, it was too late to do much in the way of stopping the course of events. That didn't stop people from noticing his actions and translating that to individuals they did not like, or that they were in direct competition with. The United States was quick to join the cause of comparing their opponents to him in hopes of gaining an advantage at the polls.

Although it was not frequent, it seemed to be predominately democrats relating Hitler with Republicans. Even before the full scope of Hitler's atrocities was known, Franklin Delano Roosevelt accused Wendell Willkie of using "Hitler Tactics" while campaigning. Willkie was a businessman and the Democrats, especially Roosevelt believed that like Hitler, Willkie would seek to control both business and government, therefore creating the atmosphere where fascism could thrive. Although in later situations you will see more of an impact, FDRs plan did little to ensure that he was eventually elected. The election was very close, but due to the conflict, and FDRs leadership and experience, Willkie lost by a slim margin. Who knows what would have happened if FDR had not said that, or if Willkie would have won, but this set up a foundation for future generations to build on.

To the best of my research, Hubert Hoover was never compared to Hitler during his presidency, which would make sense since much of his presidency Hitler was still an unknown factor. In 1946, after Hitler's death, Peter Orlov, a Russian radio commentator stated that "Hitler's friends were the Americans first."[2] This was due to Hoover calling for American neutrality during World War II. This was an asinine as the reason that Hoover did not want to become involved had nothing to do with the relationship between the United States and the Nazi Party. It was because in 1938 he "did not believe a widespread war is at all probable in the near future." He continued with, "that civilization as we know it cannot survive another great war." As the ramifications of World War I were still being felt globally.[3]

Although he did not believe that the world would enter another conflict, he was a vocal supporter of helping Nazi-occupied Europe. In fact, he was one of the main influences in creating the Commission for Polish Relief and the Finnish Relief Fund. If aiding people who were being occupied by a foreign military was "supporting" that foreign military, then I wonder if Hoover would agree with Orlov.

With the United States still reeling from the World War, the issues in Korea began and seeing a parallel to what happened in 1930s Germany, the United States believed that they had to intercede on behalf of South Korea. With the belief that so much was riding on ridding the world of fascism, the petty name calling in the United States seemed to have slowed. That was until the

---

[2] "Hoover Soviet Target," New York Times, June 23, 1946.
[3] "The Entry into Vienna Rocks Europe". *Life* 03-2- 1938, pg. 19

end of the Korean Conflict, and similar tensions in Vietnam that the invocation of Hitler began again.

Name Calling from 1960 to 2000

The first high-profile figure of the 1960s that was called Hitler was Richard Nixon in 1960 when he asked for a recount of the presidential election results. Chicago Mayor Richard Daley accused Nixon of using "Hitler-like" propaganda as the race of Nixon-Kennedy was very close. While reasonable for him to ask for a recount, the Chicago Mayor, as a Democrat, was possibly trying to discredit Nixon's intentions and connect him with someone who was still vividly in the minds of many US citizens. Hitler was power hungry but achieved his political position legally, and through the right channels. Possibly Daley felt that Nixon was power hungry and if he won would usher in a new United States, one that is against everything that Hitler stood for. Although he ultimately lost this race, he would try again, which we will get to in a bit.

Although John F. Kennedy's term as president was short, he was and still is considered one of the most loved presidents of all time. His charisma, the perpetual sense of American Optimism, and the fact he was young and had a young family all lead to his likeability. Even though he only served 1000 days, those days would to this day command a popularity unseen to this day. JFK was very charismatic and was able to bring individuals together during a turbulent period in US history. The United States was within a push of a button from going to nuclear war with the Soviet Union and Vietnam was starting to ramp up.

His popularity did not stop individuals from equating him to Hitler however. The Chinese specifically did not like Kennedy and in a New York times article, a Chinese journalist stated, "that President Kennedy surpassed Hitler and Tojo in the savagery and tyranny. Unites States imperialism is the sworn enemy of peace and the most ferocious enemy of people all over the world."[4] This is obviously a result of Kennedy's increase of troops in Vietnam being compared to Hitler's desire to expand the German empire.

Before the 1964 election, the Democratic presidential candidate George McGovern was throwing out Hitler's name to any Republican he could get it to stick to. McGovern likened Barry Goldwater, the son of a Jewish father, and a senator out of Arizona to Hitler. McGovern wasn't the only individual to compare Goldwater to Hitler. Governor Pat Brown of California stated, "Goldwater's acceptance speech had the stench of fascism. All we needed to hear was Heil Hitler." It didn't end there, with San Francisco Mayor Jack Shelley claiming that Goldwater's strategists got all of their ideas from Mein Kampf, which is the manifesto Hitler wrote while in jail.

Though Goldwater was not specifically disliked, individuals such as the NAACP leader Roy Wilkins, Martin Luther King, and George Meany of the AFL-CIO all jumped on the fascist bandwagon. The general fear was that Goldwater was leading a fear and bigotry based campaign. With as many insults flying his way, it is not surprising that he lost to Nixon in the primaries. Having achieved his goal, McGovern did not sit back, but began to amass information that he would use in 1972.

Following the death of JFK, his sitting vice-president Lyndon B. Johnson was sworn in as President. Before this however, during the 1960 election Representative William Miller likened him to Hitler due to his "Great Society" concept. Miller claimed at that proposed merger of big business with government and labor was directly comparable to Hitler's merging of big business with the government.[5] That merger assisted in Hitler gaining more traction

[4] "Kennedy Reviled by Chinese Red". *New York Times*, Sept. 27, 1962. Pg. 6
[5] *N.Y. Times*, Finney, John, Miller Attacks Big Government, Oct 28, 1964

and increased power. Since Miller had a substantial position in the United States, his usage held more clout than that of a normal citizen. One possible reason for his usage was to instantaneously cause citizens to fear or be suspicious of Johnson's actions.

This wasn't Johnson's only brush with smearing. After winning the 1964 presidential election, he subscribed to the Domino theory and containment policy for the Vietnam war. Instead of decreasing the number of troops like JFK had planned, he increased the numbers. Although unsure in the winter of 1964 regarding campaign direction, military leaders pressured him to begin a bombing campaign. In 1965 with the United States deeply embroiled in the Vietnam conflict and performing frequent air raids, various leaders began to speak out. Yugoslavian President Tito claimed that "constant air raids over Vietnam, [and] the use of a communist menace to justify turning free people into slaves of Fascism."[6]

Technically part of his comment was right, as the United States was conducting air raids, and there was a communist menace. The rest of it, however, was pure propaganda to have people believe the United States was becoming an empire, one country at a time. This fear of imperialism, especially with the issues with British Colonies, and Hitler, less than 40 years before attempting to create an empire, produced a visceral reaction. No one wanted their country to be owned by the US, especially those that were fighting to separate themselves from an imperial power. In fact, Tito's country, Yugoslavia was a young country in comparison, having formed at the end of World War I with the merger of a provisional state—that was formed from the Austro-

---

[6] *New York Times*, Binder, David Tito Likens Policy of US to Hitler's May 11, 1965

Hungarian empire — and a formerly independent country of Kingdom of Serbia.

In 1968 Nixon again ran for President of the US. During the primaries individuals were likening Nixon to Hitler frequently, this was due to many factors. Nixon ran on a platform of stability and a promise of 'Peace with Honor' in the Vietnam War. He did not release any of his specific plans, but he said he had them. It wasn't that the Democrats wanted the war to continue, but they were skeptical of Nixon's true goals. His election was very stormy, with then vice-president Hubert Humphrey declaring "If the British had not fought in 1940, Hitler would have been in London, and if the Democrats do not fight in 1968, Nixon will be in the White House." While not specifically calling him Hitler, he did directly compare Nixon to him. Humphrey did this to cause the public, especially voters to fear Nixon immediately. The tactic did not work as well as Humphrey would have liked as the election was close. By popular vote, only seven-tenths separated him from Humphrey. However, Nixon received an overwhelming number of electoral votes at 301-191-46.

McGovern, having assisted in Goldwater's loss, or at least hoping it helped, turned his vitriol on Nixon in 1972. Not only did he go directly after Nixon, but he compared policies and actions to that of the Third Reich. McGovern mentioned that he felt "the ongoing bombing campaign in Vietnam to be equal to Hitler's campaign to exterminate Jews." When the Watergate break-in occurred, McGovern stepped up again by saying "[the Watergate break-in] was the kind of thing you expect under a person like Hitler."[7] McGovern was trying to incite as much hatred and fear

---

[7] Frum, *How We Got Here*, p. 46.

in the US citizens, that there would be no chance a Republican would win the next presidential election.

McGovern was not the only individual who compared Nixon to Hitler. William Shirer, a foreign correspondent in both Europe and Asia felt that there were many comparisons between Nixon and Hitler. His comparison was from someone who was alive during Hitler's reign and saw the systematic steps that Hitler took to reach his goals. He knew that Nixon wasn't Hitler, but he feared that with the same level of compliance that the German people had for Hitler's actions, the United States could easily turn the corner. While lengthy, he points to specific events, such as the bombing of Hanoi without much outcry by the United States government or people as Nixon toeing the line of walking in Hitler's footsteps.

Shirer didn't stop there. He directly implicated Jerry Friedheim of the Pentagon as being Goebbels, Hitler's close associate and the Reich Minister of Propaganda of Nazi Germany. One of Goebbels main responsibilities was to ensure the Nazi party always looked better than the enemy by utilizing propaganda. Friedheim took a page out of Goebbels playbook by denying that the United States had damaged Hanoi's Bach Mai Hospital and told the public that it was just enemy propaganda trying to sway popular opinion.

Friedheim claimed on multiple occasions that the United States did not bomb the hospital and it was not until numerous sources provided eyewitness accounts along with video recording did Friedheim admit that while there may have been some minor accidental damage — while in actuality it was bombed out — that it was a possibility that the bombing was due to a North Vietnamese ordnance or aircraft.

Of all comparisons, Shirer's was the most educated and powerful of any of the previous attempts of comparison. Not only had Shirer actually seen the damage that Hitler had done, but he was also an observer to some of the behind the scenes events such as when Goebbels stated that not only did the Germans not sink the British liner, but that it was likely the British doing it themselves. This use of similar distraction and deflection techniques made Shirer take notice.

Another notable utterance was in 1986 when Cuban President Fidel Castro said that the President Ronald Reagan and the United States as a country were "as unscrupulous and as irresponsible as Hitler."[8] Castro even went to far as to say that Reagan was potentially more dangerous due to his control over a larger military force, one that had nuclear weapons. This was about the United States bombing Libya in response to President Reagan saying he had "irrefutable evidence that Libya was directly responsible for the West Berlin discotheque bombing that took place on April 5, 1986."[9]

The discotheque was commonly frequented by US Service Members stationed in Germany. This bombing resulted in the deaths of three individuals; two American Service Members and a Turkish woman, and injury to around 230. Immediately after the bombing, the capital of Libya, Tripoli sent an intercepted telex message to the embassy in East Berlin congratulating them on a job well done. It wasn't until the Stasi archives were opened following the reunification that names were attached to the bombing. Following six years of investigation, four individuals

---

[8] http://chicago.suntimes.com/politics/a-brief-history-of-politicians-being-compared-to-adolf-hitler/

[9] https://www.washingtonpost.com/archive/politics/1986/04/15/reagan-acted-upon-irrefutable-evidence/61170c59-b355-4e0a-8ab5-411bba4879e8/?utm_term=.ff221e48f99b

were arrested and tried. However, it was one Libyan, one German, and two Palestinians who manufactured the bomb.

The reason that Castro chose to invoke Hitler is for what he believed was American Imperialism. He believed that the United States was or would be attempting to take over other sovereign countries. Obviously, this was not the case in the discotheque bombing. There was still that small pebble of worry that Castro helped embed in Europe, Libya, and other Middle Eastern countries. What is interesting and somewhat parallel to what Tito had done was to attempt to shift the focus of the world's attention from their governments to the United States.

Throughout Reagan's presidency, the Democrats were quick to continue the Hitler analogies. Everything he did was akin to Hitler; his administration and associates were like Hitler. There was no way that Reagan could extract himself from the perceived wrongdoing. This is one of the main reasons randomly attributing actions to someone of different political ideology creates an atmosphere where it becomes almost passé. By the end of his presidency, he had been called or compared to Hitler so many times, that it was no longer shocking to him, nor was it shocking to attentive citizens.

During the same time that Ronald Reagan was compared to Hitler, the Iran-Contra affair was occurring. Oliver North, having served meritoriously in Vietnam served in various locations before attending the Command and Staff course at the Naval War College. Following his graduation in 1981, he began his assignment at the National Security Council in Washington D.C. where he served as the deputy director for the political-military affairs.

North claimed partial responsibility for the sale of weapons through intermediaries to Iran where the profits were funneled to the contras in Nicaragua. During this time, North was accused of following "Adolf Hitler's official strategy." What does this mean? Nothing really, as there was no direct comparison between Hitler's strategy and North's actions. Using Hitler's name as an insult was now so commonplace it was casually thrown around.

This rhetoric cooled down following Reagan's departure from the White House. President George H. W. Bush while invoking Hitler's name against an enemy was only slightly smeared in that fashion. In 1989 President George H.W. Bush attempted to ban flag desecration, specifically flag burning.[10] William Shirer, the same man who actively decried Nixon's actions as Third Reichesque called Bush Hitler for attempting to take away freedom of speech as outlined in the First Amendment. Beyond that, he wasn't decried as much as previous presidents. Even though he did send the United States to war, he was relatively benign in the eyes of those who were ready to voice their personal beliefs of a connection between Hitler and whoever they were opposed to.

As you can see from 1963 until the end of President George H.W. Bush's term as president the rhetoric had begun to increase with many leaders being likened to Hitler. The reasons varied from simple dislike to worries surrounding imperialism and fascist ideals. Of all those included, the one that came closest to utilizing Third Reich techniques was Nixon and his administration. Obviously, fascism did not begin in earnest, nor did Nixon seek to change his political position from President to Dictator. Following George H.W. Bush, the vitriol and labelling began to increase at a frightening speed.

---

[10] Gerstenzang, James. "Bush asks Ban on Flag Desecration: Backs Constitutional Amendment in Wake of Supreme Court Ruling." *LA Times*. June 28, 1989. http://bit.do/c7YK2

William J. Clinton was elected in hopes of changing the previous four years of Bush and republican doctrine. Initially, most were happy with the change of policy. Even though Clinton faced many issues during his presidency it did not stop opponents from criticizing how they perceived his abilities. In 2000, Clinton proclaimed that Ironwood Forest in Arizona be mandated a national park. Arizona Congressman John Shadegg compared Clinton to Hitler for his proclamation.[11]

This and the other notable example was when Jewish comedian Jackie Mason replied to an order by Clinton with, "Clinton would just as easily kill as Hitler. He has no conscience. Even if Clinton allows for one man to be killed or thousands, it is still murder." This comparison borders on obnoxious. Obviously, Clinton did not direct his cabinet to round up and kill thousands of people just because of their religion. Although the beginning of the internet age, individuals were already using it to depict Clinton as Hitler as seen in the image.

---

[11] Lazt, Marty, "The Hitler Analogy." Jewish News of Greater Phoenix, AZ, June 30, 2000. Vol. 52, issue 43; pg. 8

This name-calling was a continuation of comparing what could be construed as menial actions compared to the atrocities that Hitler committed under the Nazi Germany flag. The public was starting to hear the invocation more than before. However, the shock value was still there. The effectiveness started to wear thin when the comparison was in the vein of Clinton being referred to as Hitler over a national park. By using this insult so frequently, it became just another comment, and was largely ignored.

The other side of the Coin

Between 1960 and 1993, it was not only US political figures that were called or compared to Hitler. Political rivals and leaders do not just confine themselves to calling US citizens Hitler, no they go above and beyond that by instilling fear and disgust among the American people by comparing foreign leaders to Hitler. To justify or at least soften the proverbial blow, the US government and military have invoked the name to get something. It immediately demonizes the enemy and makes US actions seem justified. Manuel Noriega, Slobodan Milosevic, and Saddam Hussein are just three of many that the United States has publicly announced as a level of evil that demands immediate attention.

During the 1980s involving the Iran Contra affair, many in Washington D.C. were calling for a comparison between Nazi Germany and then modern day Nicaragua which was being ran by the leftist Sandinista Government. The goal was to whip the United States in such a frenzy with the belief that it was only a matter of time before Nicaragua began to spread, eventually working towards the United States. At a World's Affairs Council session in 1984, Secretary of State George Shultz said "I've had good friends who experienced Germany in the 1930s go there and come back and say, 'I've visited many communist countries, but Nicaragua doesn't feel like that. It feels like Nazi Germany.'"[12]

Not soon after that, Boston University President John Silber also compared Nicaragua's "over violence" to that of Nazi Germany's. What he failed to mention was that the United States was funding most of the aid to Contra guerrilla army therefore

---

[12] Solomon, Norman. "War Made Easy." 2005, pg.64

increasing the violent attacks. What are small things like aiding the death of people when you can liken them to Hitler.

It didn't take long for the United States to be at the precipice of another conflict. On August 2, 1990 Iraq invaded Kuwait under the leadership of Saddam Hussein. In preparation for military action, President Bush began comparing Hussein to Hitler. The white house put out a message from Bush that stated "A half century ago our nation and the world paid dearly for appeasing an aggressor who should, and could, have been stopped. We are not going to make the same mistake again."

Even though many journalists responded with opposition to the comparison, stating that it would create unneeded hysteria and confusion. The White House and Bush did not care, they wanted the hysteria to be there. In fact, within three weeks of this comment, his popularity rose from 58 percent to 76 percent. The support gave room for military deployment.

The LexisNexus, a database that provides legal, governmental, business, and high-tech information, found that during the Congressional election and the five months following the invasion, American news outlets used the comparison between Hussein and Hitler several times a day. This allowed the public to be consistently bombarded with the comparison, causing exactly what the White House administration wanted.

The thing is, Hussein was never a kind leader, he was always a fierce dictator. Until the invasion of Kuwait, Hussein had been on good terms with the United States. So good that the during the Iran-Iraq war that spanned most of the 80s, the US government provided tangible assistance to Hussein and Iraq. While the White House waited until the invasion to flip the proverbial Hitler switch, there had been some inkling that a similarity existed. An influential magazine displayed Hussein's face with the now unforgettable mustache that Hitler is known for.

It seems like it is only during war time that the United States political leaders start comparing possible enemies with Hitler. In 1995, after roughly four years of fighting the Croatian Army, express approval by the United States entered the Krajina region of then Croatia and Bosnia and Herzegovina. The results were devastating, with over 150,000 Serbian people being removed from their homes.

Initially, both the White House and news outlets were essentially mum on the issue. The White House had said this was an internal issue and that it would get figured out. It wasn't something that Americans should worry about. Other media sources were not so keen to shrug it off. BBC correspondent Misha Glenny wrote that "The entire offensive was undertaken by the Authorities in Zagreb with the support of the United States government." She did not end there, however, but continued, "If we accept that it is all right for Tudjman to cleanse Croatia of its Serbs, then how on earth can we object if [Boris] Yeltsin cleanses Chechnya or if one day Milosevic sends his army to clean the Albanians from Kosovo." She was more prophetic then I am sure she wanted to be.

Just like with Hussein the tides do turn. When Milosevic began to cleanse Kosovo, the US military decided to protect those that just earlier they were okay with being killed. President Clinton gave a speech the day before the United States began to bomb the Serbian Nationalists. He said "And so I want to talk to you about Kosovo today, but just remember this –it's about our values. What if someone had listened to Winston Churchill and stood up to Adolf Hitler earlier?"

The longer the bombing run continued, the more Clinton and White House staff connected Milosevic to Nazi Germany and Hitler. This not only gave the United States morale ground for the bombing, but gave a face to the enemy. Few knew what Milosevic looked like, but everyone knew what Hitler looked like. As the bombing continued, the rhetoric did as well. Vice President Al Gore called him "one of these junior league Hitler types". That doesn't make sense, and it just to connect the two names. Other government officials called what Milosevic was doing just short of genocide.

This time, however, there was an outcry of how preposterous it was to compare Yugoslavia with Nazi Germany, but not for the reasons many may think. A Washington Post staff, Michael Dobbs reported that "Any comparison between the rump, Serb-led Yugoslavia and Nazi Germany is laughable." He believed that Yugoslavia was so weak and poor that no one should really pay them of mind, while Nazi Germany was powerful, and had enemies cowering in fear.

As can be seen, the years from 1960 to 2000 were starting to display the way Hitler's name was used to get something desired. Be it the presidency, or to give a reason to engage in war, Hitler's name was used sparingly with a marked increase during Clinton's tenue. This sparse usage ensured that when used, it would impact the desired recipients; citizens, other leaders, Congress with the utmost impact. It ensured that whatever the intent was, it would come to reality. This included winning elections or engaging in war when it was beneficial. By the end of Clinton's presidency, the initial shock value of the invocation had started to dull. However, as it was not used extensively, there was still power in words.

Ramp Up 2000-2016

The rhetoric including Hitler that existed before 2000 could be considered sparse, paltry even, compared to the amount that occurred during the presidency's of George W. Bush and Barrack Obama. There wasn't a clear-cut reason behind an increased use, however, the term "Hitler" was constantly repeated on all media formats, be it radio, newsprint, or television. It could be because more people were studying World War II, but the issue with that is the comparisons were only for fear-mongering, without actual reason or information to back up the claims, very unlike what is currently transpiring in the United States. If you dig enough, there will always be some connection, such as the game six degrees of Kevin Bacon. Could it be that all the recognizable actors are in the same movies, or could it be that he has been in so many movies that no matter how hard it may seem, if you dig deep, there will be a connection. One must be careful not to lose sight of objectivity when you are desperately trying to find that comparison, or connection.

One reason that many felt that both George W. Bush and Barack Obama were compared more frequently, and with more intensity than anyone in the past was due to social media and the expansion of the internet. Bloggers, journalists, and anyone with a computer could write whatever they wanted without it being reviewed by an editor, or checked for accuracy. With photo altering programs becoming less expensive, it is no wonder that images of these two presidents were transformed into Hitler. Even though everyone and anyone could claim a direct link, there was no actual evidence that either men's actions were similar to those of Adolf Hitler. Again, it was used for shock value, but like with many things, the more it is used, the less it is listened to. Not unlike the boy who cried wolf.

There is an old saying about the sins of the father, and when George W. Bush, the son of the previous president George H.W. Bush was elected president, some of the same comparisons were used to connect son to father. Within a year of Bush's inauguration, 19 Middle Eastern terrorists hijacked four planes and committed the single largest terrorist act on American soil. Two planes were diverted and flown into the Twin Towers, part of the World Trade Center in New York City. One was flown into the Pentagon, and the fourth, due to passengers actively engaging the Hijackers, crashed in a field in Pennsylvania.

Following the terrorist attack, On October 7, 2001, President Bush reacted by declaring war on Afghanistan. It was believed that all 19 terrorists were part of al-Qaida, which was thought to be primarily based in Afghanistan. The goal was to find and kill the suspected leader, Osama Bin Laden. Shortly after Christmas 2001 when Bush was at his house in Texas, he was briefed on the events, including the fact that Bin Laden escaped capture. Interestingly, Bush was not particularly interested in Bin Laden. He kept asking about Saddam Hussein and what the situation was in Iraq. It became apparent that Bush had already set his eyes on Iraq as the next target. At the same briefing General Franks formally briefed Bush, Cheney, and the other members on plans for Desert Storm II, which they had been planning for since the middle of November.

Less than a month after this briefing, on January 29, 2002, President Bush gave a State of the Union address that began to publicly focus on Iraq as an "axis of evil" even though an al-Qaeda arm based in Afghanistan were behind the attack on the World Trade Center. It was apparent that Bush's strategy mirrored that of his father's regarding Iraq and Hussein. His justification was that Iraq and Hussein had Weapons of Mass Destruction (WMDs). He came to this conclusion after a haphazard collection of CIA information, including opinions, and estimations regarding Hussein's inventory of biological and nuclear weapons, and if Iraq had directly assisted Bin Laden was boiled down to a one page brief. To this day there is speculation on rather Iraq really had WMDs or if this was just a farce to allow the United States government to declare war on a father's grudge.

Regardless of the real reason for invading Iraq, on March 20, 2003, the United States and more than 30 of its allies invaded Iraq and quickly defeated the Iraqi Military. On April 9, 2003, Baghdad fell, and on May 1, 2003, onboard the USS Abraham Lincoln, president Bush had a "mission accomplished" speech. Obviously, his speech was premature, as the stability of Iraq continued to deteriorate. In the years that followed, more than 3,000 American troops, and an unknown Iraqi population would lose their lives in attempts to quell uprisings.

Even though Bush and his administration were adamant that a troop decrease would be detrimental, Congress, and allies began to worry about the long-term cost of staying in Iraq. On January 10, 2007, Bush asked for an increase of 21,500 American troops along with a job program for Iraqis and additional construction proposals to the tune of 1.2 billion dollars. Congress was becoming increasingly concerned about the situation and opposed both the surge and the additional money. In response, Bush asked for just an additional 8,000 troops. Instead of receiving additional troops, what Bush did was to extend those who were currently deployed to Iraq while not pushing the deployment of incoming troops back. This allowed a double up on some bases that were critical to sustaining what he believed was the upper hand in the ongoing conflict.

For much of President Bush's time in office, Democrats and foreign leaders would jump to compare him to Hitler. Initially, it was left leaning outspoken individuals who jumped at the chance to nail Bush with the same moniker that his father was called. Kurt Vonnegut quipped, "The only difference between Bush and Hitler is that Hitler was elected." Obviously, history tells a different story and Hitler was not elected, and Bush was, although he lost the popular vote.

Both Al Gore, the politician that lost to Bush in the 2000 Presidential election, and Congressman Keith Ellison compared the attack on the world trade center buildings to Nazi Germany. Gore claimed that the "Administration works closely with a network of rapid-response digital Brown Shirts." Which was another moniker for Nazi Germany soldiers as they wore brown. Ellison, part of the 9/11 truthers movement compared the attack to the Reichstag fire. The Reichstag fire was a fire that was set by a Dutch communist. Hitler used this event to suspend civil liberties to counter what he said was a growing communist issue in Germany. This will be discussed in depth in part two.

They were not the last to compare Bush's actions to those of Hitler, or to members of Nazi Germany's leadership. Another Democrat, Senator Robert Byrd, a former Klansman, compared Bush to Hermann Goering, one of Hitler's military leaders, and the second most powerful men in Nazi Germany. The comparison is weak and feels like an attempt to try to take Bush out at the knees. Goering was a military expert, having created both the Gestapo and leading the Luftwaffe until the last days of World War II. I guess the fact that both men were pilots made the comparison somewhat viable.

There seemed to be nothing that President Bush could do to absolve himself of the comparison. In 2002 during the German elections, a justice minister, Herta Daubler-Gmelin said "Bush wants to divert attention from his domestic problems. It's a classic tactic. It's one that Hitler also used."[13] This sparked a small amount of outrage from the United States, but in Germany, the comment, and the reason behind it was used in attempts of discrediting Daubler-Gmelin's boss during a contentious election cycle. Daubler-Gmelin replied by saying that she, "didn't compare the persons Bush and Hitler, but their methods." This seems plausible and factually accurate. Both Hitler and Bush had domestic issues, which they tried to divert from. The war in Iraq was a very good diversion tool.

John Kerry joined the presidential race in 2003 as the Democratic nominee against Bush, who was running for reelection. Moveon.org ran a contest at the end of 2003 and early 2004 for amateur ads against President Bush. Among the 1,500 videos submitted there were some that spliced images of Hitler and Bush together. Having received far more than anticipated, Moveon.Org staff posted all the videos on their contest website. Soon after the initial posting of the ads, leaders of the nonprofit not only removed the ads but denounced their content.

It was already too late, as Bush's campaign had seen them and were outraged that there were images of Hitler and the Nazi party associated with an American President, not like it hadn't been done before, but alas Moveon.org apologized and ensured that none of them remained. His campaign staff believed that the only response would be to create a video denouncing John Kerry as being associated with Hitler-like tactics.

---

[13] Erlanger, Steven. "Bush-Hitler remark shows U.S. as issue in German Election." *The New York Times*. Sept. 30, 2002. Accessed at http://nyti.ms/2jFXHzW

When confronted with their video, the GOP and campaign staff insisted that they were just trying to show what the Democrats were putting in front of the voting public, and to denounce all Nazi Party connections. The video shows pieces of the moveon.org video as well as clips of Kerry supporters who were upset and angry at actions that Bush had involved the United States with. Even though the connection that Bush attempted was laughable, many of supporters, however, paid into the belief that Kerry was somehow directly responsible for the original Bush, Hitler ad, even though there was zero proof to support that.[14]

With the internet being widely accessible, images of Bush as Hitler began to emerge by the handful. Some were in direct response to events, while others were just because it was easy, and hopefully the image would somehow change an opinion of belief, which it is unlikely that occurred. This accessibility also led to a possible connection between the President George W. Bush's Grandfather and Hitler, which lead to more frenzied image creation such as the one below. To this day people are trying to either prove, or disprove that there was a connection between Adolf Hitler and Prescott Bush.

---

[14] The video in question can be viewed at http://bit.ly/2kyMRzZ.

In 2002 and 2003, directly following the invasion of Iraq, there seemed to be images of Bush likened to Hitler everywhere. Some believed that Bush was the incarnation of Hitler and so they created imagery that portrayed Bush as Hitler, with both the signature mustache and with a visible swastika. One individual took it even further and added the swastika to the S in Bush's last name as seen in the following image.

Others wanted to show a similarity while comparing the two men. An image detailing the two events, the Reichstag fire and 9/11 questioned the path Bush was taking. It was seen as the beginning of tighter controls on civil liberties, and start of a reign of terror. There are some people to this day that believe 9/11 was orchestrated just to enable the United States to engage in warfare in hopes to strengthening a weak economy. Rather it was or not; the economy did bounce a little among companies that provide items for military use.

The problem is, Bush was like Hitler due to Bush's actions. Does that make him Hitler? No, but his actions were reminiscent of those of the Nazi Party. Although there are many more comparisons, there are four that jump to my mind that not only compare Bush to Hitler, but also Trump to Hitler. More on Trump's comparison to Hitler later. One of the most important was that like Hitler, the majority did not elect either Bush or Trump, but were forced to engage in political maneuvering to gain office. Like Hitler, both Bush and Trump began to curtail civil liberties in response to a well-publicized disaster. Hitler used the Reichstag fire, while Bush and Trump used 9/11, with Trump throwing in the Syrian refugee issue.

Additionally; Hitler, Bush, and Trump all pursued a reckless foreign policy without the mandate of the electorate and despite the opposition of most foreign nations. The last on this list, but not the last comparison is that like Hitler, Bush and Trump displayed great populist enthusiasm in patriotic speeches, but primarily serves wealthy investors who subsidize his election campaigns and share with him their lifestyle. See how when broken down the similarities can be terrifying.

It was getting to the point that anything could invoke Hitler's name, and the Democrats and other left-leaning parties were using it to their full advantage. Whereas before, Hitler comparisons were used sparingly and with regards to specific events or topics that closely mimicked that of Nazi Germany. With Bush's presidency, the United States began to see any small or otherwise inconsequential event that was against those of the liberal parties were akin to Nazism.

It became second nature to throw Bush's name in with Hitler's. The public was becoming immune to the intense reaction that Hitler and Nazi could invoke. Optimists on both political sides hoped and truly believed that Bush would be the pentacle of Hitler comparisons and after Bush leaves the Oval office, the rhetoric would die down.

Although many thought and hoped that with the transition from Bush to whoever was elected in 2008 the name calling, and image creation would die down. This was especially the case with those Democrats or other left leaning individuals who would likely have control over the Oval Office with how Bush's eight years had gone. Even after President Bush was out of office, it did not stop people from comparing and contrasting Bush with Hitler.

In 2014, some six years after Bush left the White House, a sixth-grade teacher in Washington D.C. assigned her students a project to make comparisons using a Venn diagram between Bush and Hitler that stated: "Both men abused their powers." Parents complained that was disrespectful to the Presidential position, and the teacher and school district offered a formal apologize.[15]

With the election and the victory of not only a Democrat, but an African American Democrat, those who so adamantly referred to Bush and Hitler felt they could breathe a little easier. They believed that no one would attribute elements of Hitler onto an African American.

President Barack Obama entered the White House as not only a popular vote and electoral college victor, but also as the first African American President. Many people voted for him in hopes of leaving the Middle East peacefully and without additional bloodshed. As he was the first African American, there was bound to be some issues among the White Supremacist population in the United States, but were usually hesitate to compare him to Hitler, for obvious reasons.

While historically it has been shown that democrats, or those who were more liberal than others could jump at the chance to compare Hitler to their opponents, with President Obama, it was the republicans who became almost obsessed with comparing Obama with Hitler.

Within a month of Obama being elected, Glenn Beck, an ardent conservative began what would be a steady stream of Hitler-Obama comparisons. Obama came into office and began to create legislation that many saw as removing citizen's rights, similar to what Hitler did in 1933. Obama was within his right as president to create executive orders that he and his administration believed were in the best interest of the nation. Obviously not everyone was going to agree with that sentiment. Within a year of

---

[15] Sarahtr, "Teacher to students: Compare George W. Bush to Hitler." Chicago Sun Times, September 11, 2014. Found at http://bit.ly/2k2bbqF

his election, not only had Beck thrown out some comparisons, but so had Rush Limbaugh and Ben Carson.

Why was he so hated that nothing he could do would break him out of the Hitler mold? Part of it was the belief that his campaign slogans of "change" and his push to increase the number of voters in the United States, something that everyone should want, would be directly attributed to something Hitler would do if he was alive. Of the three, Ben Carson's statements were the most telling. "[Obama's administration is] very much like Nazi Germany, … you had the government using its tools to intimidate the population. We now live in a society where people are afraid to say what they actually believe."[16] His reasoning was the increased nature of political correctness and what he believed was government intimidation. When coupled, it prevents open and honest dialogue. If one was to examine the multitude of websites dedicated to out crying Obama's policy changes, it is hard to see where speech was curtailed.

Not only were political rivals and bloggers online throwing insults and comparisons, but someone familiar with the Nazi Party spoke out. A holocaust survivor began to tour the United States speaking on behalf of many conservatives that she believes Obama will usher in another Nazi Germany. She spoke on points such as gun control and tax reformation that Obama had campaigned on. Her speeches were just what people who already believed this wanted to hear. Here was a woman who survived Nazi Germany explaining exactly how Hitler slowly gained power and control over the entire country. There was even a time when an email of her explaining in detail the takeover circulated. For someone who was already leaning towards Obama being the

---

[16]"Exclusive – Dr. Ben Carson: Our Government is like "Nazi Germany." Breitbart TV. Found at http://bit.ly/2kFDUol

second Hitler, her email was the confirmation needed. For others, her email read as anecdotical and opinion based.

Not unlike previous presidents, there were the fringe individuals and groups who created websites and other talking points about how Obama was the new Hitler, from his slogan of "forward", to outlandish claims that because the two men held outdoor rallies and that they originally had different last names they were similar. If you take that into account, certain politicians, actors, and musicians would be the next Hitler. Remember the note about digging enough. This is was true as ever with Obama.

In January 2015 France held a unity march in remembrance of the 17 individuals who died during three days of deadly attacked in Paris. The White House initially declined to send someone, and Representative Randy Weber, a Texas Republican immediately took to Twitter to voice his displeasure. "Even Adolph Hitler thought it was more important than Obama to get to Paris. (For all the wrong reasons.) Obama couldn't do it for the right reasons." It had become commonplace to attribute Hitler like characteristics whenever someone may disagree with you. The White House did send someone, and John Kerry, the sitting Secretary of State, went.

It did not take long for the Democrats to lash out at Weber for what was perceived a faux pas, although as can been seen it was the Democrats who usually started the Hitler comparisons. Due to the backlash from both peers and Twitter users, Weber issued an apology the next day stating that he didn't mean to trivialize the Holocaust nor to compare the President to Hitler. It would not be the last time that politician would use Hitler for their benefit.

In July of the same year Mike Huckabee took the comparison further than others by stating the Iran nuclear deal was akin to marching the Israelis to the door of the oven. He claimed that many Jewish individuals have been overall agreeable to his comparison. While this was not the 10th or 100th time that those more conservative of the nation would compare Obama to Hitler, this one took it a bit further. By pulling in those who were normally very adamant about not agreeing Hitler analogies, the statement by Huckabee was surprising to say the least.

Reddit, an online community recently created a spreadsheet of the number of times that Hitler was mentioned in a subreddit titled Worldnews. In February 2008 when President Obama had been in office for a month there were 6 references to Hitler. As time went on the mentions increased and stayed between 50 and 500 until August 2012. At that point, they began to increase and for the most part stay above 1000 mentions a month until the graph ends on November 2016.[17] There were substantial spikes March 2014 with 3388, August 2014 with 3015, and July 2016 with 3435. A Reddit user made this graph, and is not meant to be scientific as there are many variables associated with who, why, and when the mentions occurred. What it does show, however, is that compared to one or two instances a year, the expansion of the internet allowed an increase of individuals who invoke Hitler, possibly without having a legitimate reason for doing so.

The imagery that was published during his campaign and terms in office added to the conversation on how "Hitleresque" Obama was compared to Hitler himself. In 2008 Obama's campaign was change with the O being a road of sorts. That prompted this image by those who believe that Obama was going to socialize the United States with universal healthcare and caring about everyone which is interesting since Hitler did not care for everybody, only those who he felt were part of the Master race.

---

[17] "Dataisbeautiful," *Reddit*. Found at http://bit.ly/2kCKfkL

When this type of imagery did not receive the response that was hoped for, those who wanted the world to know exactly how they felt stepped up their game. This image not only had Obama resembling Hitler, but also the Iron Cross and the Swastika both on a flag and on a lapel pin. If anyone had any doubt that Obama was following in Hitler's footsteps this image erased all doubt.

Towards the end of Obama's second term it became apparent that the voracity and quantity of comparisons were unparalleled to any previous president or politician. History may in fact prove those individuals right that policy wise Obama was the closest president to Nazi Germany, or will show that all of those who spent more time attempting to draw comparisons than actively assisting the rebuilding of the United States. Instead they participated either directly or indirectly in the growing divide between the liberal and conservative population. Many believe that never before had a president's legitimate occupation, the presidency, been questioned as much as Obama's had. In fact some still do not believe that Obama was a US born citizen, including the newly elected president, Donald Trump.

Obviously, some of those mentions were targeting President Obama, but others were likely aimed at the 2016 Presidential election candidates. The 2016 election was contentious and full of rhetoric that not only targeted an individual, but at times an entire party. Most notably both presidential candidates Hillary Clinton and Donald Trump were on the front lines of this particularly nasty smear campaign. As to not repeat information about Donald Trump, his campaign and early presidency will be discussed in the second part of this book.

Hillary Clinton, the wife of former President William Clinton, became the Democratic nominee for the 2016 Presidential election. The closer it got to the November election, the more information was presented against Clinton's bid for president. Formerly the Secretary of State under President Obama, there were many groups that did not believe she should be president. While most Hitler insult-throwing individuals were firmly against Trump, there were those who believed that Clinton embodied Hitler-like tendencies much more.

On October 30, 2016, Louis Farrakhan, the leader of the Nation of Islam compared Clinton to Hitler during a sermon. He stated that "Of course she apologized, but just a minute. See, Hitler could've said to the Jews after Auschwitz, 'I'm so sorry.' Would that be enough to satisfy you?"[18] Obviously, the question was rhetorical but it brings up a good point on how apologies should be looked at. This comment related back to when Clinton had spoken in support of a crime bill that her husband, President Clinton had signed in 1994. Apparently, she called the young African American men and women "super predators" and needed to be "brought to heel". She later apologized for the remark, but by that point it was too late in Farrakhan's eyes.

With how contentious the election was, it is no surprise that individuals spoke of all the attributes Clinton had that resembled those of Hitler. Things such as gun control, taxation, Economic policy and even abortions were used to compare the two. While the right lapped up the comparisons, this goes back to being able to find a correlation between two individuals if you dig enough. Let's take economic policy for example. The argument as that both Clinton and Hitler liked public works programs, like building bridges and roads. Yes, the fact that Clinton wanted better roads and bridges tagged her as being like Hitler. Apparently, that means for the leader of the United States to not be like Hitler; they must hate public works projects and only hire private companies.

---

[18] "Farrakhan compares Hillary Clinton to Hitler in Sermon." Foxnews.com, found at http://fxn.ws/2fx4Y8H

See how convoluted and thin the comparisons could be to bring about fear and hatred.

Not unlike her husband, Clinton, during her presidential campaign saw images depicting her as Hitler. Her attitude towards society as opposed to individual rights also contributed to the comparison. She may have been a lot of things, but the second coming of Hitler was not one of them. As can be seen, the name calling and even loosely creating connections were mostly just white noise during the election. Overall the comparisons between Clinton and Hitler were few, as her emails were of much more importance. That didn't stop some conservatives from creating images like the one below.

2016 saw a heightened level of political awareness and name calling, not just from the political opponents but also from voters, journalists, and the public. While interesting from a sociological point of view, the gap between the liberal side and conservative side was expanding. It would need a president that could speak to both sides, and was not polarizing to bring the country back together.

The years from 2000 to 2016 not only saw an increase in the polarization of the country along the political line, but a noticeable uptick in the number of times "Hitler" was used online and in the media. To be fair, it wasn't always a political rival contributing to the rhetoric but foreign dignitaries. Foreign leaders were not immune from being labeled. What is important to note is the reason foreign leaders were likened to Hitler. The reasons are not as clear-cut as they appear.

Who isn't like Hitler?

During President George H.W. Bush's presidency it was imperative that Hussein was likened to Hitler to gain public support for justifying the 1990 invasion of Iraq. After the attack on the World Trade Center, it did not take long for President George W. Bush to pull up old grudges, and use the same script to justify war with Iraq again.

By 2002, Hussein had not instigated war with another country since 1990, and his military's abilities were mediocre at best. This did not stop Bush and his administration from pulling out the old comparison of Hussein to Hitler. Christopher Shays, considered a moderate Republican, repeatedly invoked Hitler and the Third Reich to justify the invasion. In fact, only days before the resolution of war, Shays went on MSNBC and used a direct comparison between Hussein and Hitler in hopes of swaying public and political opinions. When asked about the weapons of mass destruction, Shays shuffled and avoided.

> "We're not talking about a criminal act that we have to prove in court. We're talking about the logic of events. Someone said to me, 'Prove that he will use his nuclear weapons.' To me, that's like saying, 'Prove Hitler's Germany was going to go into Poland.' We knew he went into Czechoslovakia. We knew he went into Austria. We knew he was building up his armament. We knew what he was about. We could never have proved he was going into Poland."[19]

That makes sense in a twisted way. It is the devil you don't know versus the devil you do. In other words, it is better to jump

---

[19] Solomon, Norman. "'This guy is a Modern-Day Hitler.'" Alternet.org. Found at http://bit.ly/1qPpRw3

the gun, then to let the gun go off in your face. We have seen that it is usually the Democrats who are quick to compare opponent candidates, or enemies to Hitler, and Tom Lantos, the ranking Democrat did not differ. Lantos was not to be beat in comparisons. In October 2002, Lantos spoke on Capitol Hill, "Had Hitler's regime been taken out in a timely fashion, the 51 million innocent people who lost their lives during the Second World War would have been able to finish their normal life cycle. Mr. Chairman, if we appease Saddam Hussein, we will stand humiliated before both humanity and history."[20] In other words, Hussein was Hitler, and do not be surprised if another 51 million lives were taken if we, the United States does not step in immediately.

When supporters of the invasion were called to task regarding the lack of WMDs and other revelations, they upped their rhetoric to ensure that no one would pull funding and troop support. Jay Garner, when asked to speak to the House Subcommittee, which he anticipated was going to be a challenge; he came prepared. When criticized about how the administration handled the Iraq war so far, Garner related his own experience seeing children's bodies being pulled from Saddam's 'killing fields.' Garner also directly compared Hussein not only to Hitler but to the Cambodian leader, Pol Pot, who was also responsible for the deaths of approximately 25 percent of the Cambodian population during his reign.

Incidentally, the killing fields that Garner invoked for outrage were mostly created when the United States supported him, both in the 1970s when he was combating communists and in the 1980s when he slaughtered tens of thousands during the Iraq-Iran

---

[20] Opinion Piece, "Rhetoric Starts Here." Washington Post. Full article found here: http://wapo.st/2kLD8Dq

conflict. It was only after Hussein was no longer useful to the United States that these killing fields were discussed.

During the time when comparisons were flying between Hitler and Hussein, there were also comparisons between Hitler and Bin Laden. President Bush compared Bin Laden to Hitler during a speech to United States military leaders. On September 5, 2006, Bush was quoted as saying, "Underestimating the words of evil and ambitious men is a terrible mistake." As he spoke, he referred to Bin Laden and al-Qaeda members. "In the 1920s a failed Austrian painter published a book in which he explained his intention to build an Aryan superstate in Germany and take revenge on Europe and eradicate the Jews — The world ignored Hitler's words and paid a terrible price."[21] He was trying to push people to not only agree with him, but to understand that words and thoughts should not be overlooked. "Bin Laden and his terrorist have made their intentions as clear as Lenin and Hitler before them." This is his way of comparing the two without saying "Bin Laden is Hitler," possibly understanding that direct comparisons may turn some people away, but by inferring, listeners can it however they want.

It was not only political leaders naming Bin Laden as Hitler, but there were articles written on the comparisons. National Geographic wrote an article on October 19, 2011, on "The Eeriest Parallel: Hitler and Osama [Bin Laden]." Their main comparisons were how people felt after both men died exactly 66 years apart, under what could be considered unverifiable ways. Hitler killed himself in a bunker and many believed that he in fact survived and moved to Argentina or anywhere other than Europe and the

---

[21] "Bush compares Bin Laden to Hitler," September 5, 2006, Speech, found at http://news.bbc.co.uk/2/hi/5318204.stm.

United States. When Bin Laden was killed, they verified his death by photographs and analysis of his DNA.

The other comparison that National Geographic mentions is how psychologically both men were similar in that they both believed they were their people's messiahs. Experts believe that Hitler thought himself as the Aryan race's messiah and that he was going to propel them to the top. Bin Laden, likewise, saw himself as the messiah of not only the Muslim people, but perhaps even humanity. Other individuals that were included were cult leaders who have the same sense of messiahship.[22]

Did Hussein and Bin Laden have some of the same traits that Hitler had? Of course, they did. Both men wanted to set their country or organization apart and above the rest of the world. Hitler believed that the Aryan race should be the wealthiest and strongest, therefore revered by all others. If that took killing those opposed to them, then that is what they would do to make sure their goals were achieved. Like with earlier comparisons, specifically those of who the United States considered an enemy, the comparison is only used to frighten the public and decision makers at the government level to go along with condemnation or to agree to a military invasion. This harkening back to Hitler and the 1930s is just wordplay, and it is unknown if even Bush and others truly believed what they were saying.

The throwing around of Hitler's name elevated to the point of almost being laughable when in 2010 Georgia's State Representative John Yates said Illegal immigrants are like Hitler and should be shot. His reasoning was that like Hitler, they're enemies of the United States. He went on say that "Stopping Hitler was worth the price, ...It's our border, they're invading

---

[22] Kiger, Patrick J. "The Eeriest Parallel." *National Geographic.* October 19, 2011. Found online at http://on.natgeo.com/2jZT8Ec

us."[23] It would seem Yates had not picked up a history book in a while to believe that individuals seeking a better life were akin to a man who sought to kill those individuals that he felt would diminish the good name of Germany.

It is no surprise that Vladimir Putin was compared to Hitler, with his attacks on neighboring countries, and his desire to ensure 'ethnic Russians' are safe in whatever country they may live in. What is surprising is that it was Hillary Clinton at a private fundraising in Long Beach, California who did so. In 2014 Vladimir Putin began to worry about the safety of Russians living in European countries and so he began to issue Russian passports to Ukrainian citizens, some began to get worried.

Clinton comparing Putin to Hitler said, "Now if this sounds familiar, it's what Hitler did back in the '30s." She continued, "All the Germans that were…the ethnic Germans, the German by ancestry who were in places like Czechoslovakia and Romania and other places, Hitler kept saying they're not being treated right. I must go and protect my people, and that's what's gotten everyone so nervous."[24] Others shared her concern, but not her exact phrasing.

By 2014 when Clinton said this, most people knew the "who's Hitler next" game, and so did not take her and the statement seriously. Yes, there were similarities as some reporters pointed out, but many believed that Putin, if he was to decide on seeking world domination akin to Hitler, there would be enough power arranged against him that he and Russia would be easily containable. Obviously still dangerous, but as Putin is believed to

---

[23] Webster, Stephen, "GOP Lawmaker: Illegal immigrants are like 'Hitler', should be shot." *Rawstory*. Found at http://bit.ly/2jN4vvN

[24] "Hillary Clinton's Putin-Hitler Analogy." BBC News, March 6, 2014. Found at http://bbc.in/1qcHlOs

be an opportunist, the minute strong opposition presented itself, he would back down. Could this be hopeful thinking? Possibly, but with the current political and military situations occurring in the world, hopefully, it is also rational thinking.

US politicians were not the only ones subjected to random, and at times adamant Hitler comparisons. Internationally, those who had drastically different opinions or political motivations were also compared. At times, it was to garner anger towards an individual such as attacks against Putin. Other times, a slow and subconscious change to how the public felt about a individual. Using Hitler to compare to both Hussein and Bin Laden made going to war a little easier to swallow. If a politician or group starts to refer to a foreign individual as Hitler, or comparing the two, be mindful that a request for intervention and war may be on the horizon.

The importance of this part was to detail the evolution of Hitler comparisons, and why they were increasingly used from WWII until present. One may think, "Oh the same is true for why they call Trump Hitler, or why someone may compare the two." That is not the case at all, in fact, the actions of President Trump in the year leading up to the 2016 election and of the months following the election tell a different story. It tells a story that could fundamentally change the future of the United States for generations to come.

Part Two: Hitler and Trump

From the beginning

As you can see in the past there were leaders, and other influential individuals that were likened to Hitler. However, it wasn't until the election cycle for the 2016 Presidency that there was a candidate that slowly but surely began to use direct elements of Mein Kompf to not only get the Republican nominee for President, but to also win the presidency on the premise of "for the people".

One thing that is important to note, that while Hitler did horrible things, and can be considered a horrible human being, he did have some "redeeming qualities" such as his ability to command a group, and the charisma that was needed for it. Trump is no different, he does have debatably excellent business and financial sense, and the charisma to move a crowd.

As there isn't just one or two comparable actions between Trump and Hitler, each chapter will consist of a single aspect of comparison as opposed to earlier where a paragraph was used. Why is this? Bluntly speaking, the actions that have occurred in the last four months have shown that while Hitler took years to shape his and Germany's future, Trump is using days with the help of some individuals who may not always have Trump's or the United States' best interests in mind.

Not all of the comparisons are directly Trump as the people who he appointed and nominated also have fascist tendencies. The people that Hitler, and now Trump surrounded themselves with tell a lot more about the leader than strictly their policies and opinions. Hitler could not have done it without key members, just as Trump is unable to do with without his supporting staff.

Hitler's background is briefly discussed in Part One, but there is much more that makes him who he was. Adolf Hitler was born in 1889 in what now is Austria near Linz. He moved to Germany in 1913 and joined the German army during World War I. Following the war, Hitler was appointed as a special commando to assign German soldiers to infiltrate the German Worker's Party(DAP). While monitoring the soldiers and the DAP, Hitler was drawn to the founder Anton Drexler's ideas. These ideas were anti-Semitic, nationalist, anti-capitalist, and anti-marxist in nature and fit what Hitler was already starting to believe. Drexler, impressed with Hitler's ability to command attention with his speaking style formally invited him to the DAP. It was not long before Hitler joined on September 12, 1919.

***

Donald J. Trump was born June 1946 in New York City. His father was of German ancestry, and his mother was from Scottish ancestry. His paternal side were wealthy, with his Grandfather amassing the family fortune operating restaurants and boarding houses around Seattle and Klondike Canada during the height of the gold rush. His father used some of that wealth to become a New York real estate developer. Trump's mother immigrated from Scotland and became a maid prior to meeting and marrying Trump's father.

Trump attended a military academy and then college at both the Fordham University and Wharton School, but did not serve in the military, receiving both student deferrals and medical deferrals during the Vietnam conflict. He has since written that his medical deferrals were due to bone spurs in his heels.

Following college, Trump began working for the family business and married and divorced two women. He had four children between the two marriages. His third marriage produced one child and he is currently still married. He has been quoted as saying that the first two marriages ended due to his commitment to the business and that his first two wives were unable to compete with his love of work.

Prior to 2000, Trump had amassed a net worth of more than one billion dollars due to his business ventures and the sale of his name for branding purposes according to him. Forbes and other financial publications claim this number is much lower. In 2000 Trump filed an exploratory committee to seek a presidential nomination by the reform party. Polls stated that against the Republican George W. Bush, and the Democrat Al Gore he could see as much as seven percent of the final votes. Due to party infighting, Trump removed himself from candidacy, although by this point he had already won California and Michigan's party nomination during the spring primaries.

Trump considered running again as a Republican in 2012 but ultimately decided against it. In July 2015 Trump announced his candidacy for the President of the United States as a republican. His speech was highlighted with domestic issues such as illegal immigration, offshoring of American jobs, the national debt, and Islamic terrorism. He stood by these issues and his slogan for the campaign was "Make America Great Again."

During the initial months following his announcement he began to claim that he disdained political correctness and that the media was intentionally misinterpreting his words, this began his attacks on the main stream media. When Spencer coined "alt-right in 2000, he defined it as a white nationalist movement, and is comprised of individuals with far-right ideologies. Those who are against the term, believe that it is used to white wash overt racism, Nazism, and white supremacy. In fact Spencer has frequently spoken of propaganda used by the Nazis and many of his talks have an anti-Semitic feel to them.

Since Trump's nomination as the republican presidential nominee, alt-right has been considered antisemitism, neo-nazism, nativism, Islamophobia, antifeminism, homophobia, white nationalism, right-wing populism, and the neoreactionary movement. Most importantly though, is that those who claim to be part of the alt-right movement have publicly backed Trump's nomination for president. In fact, Trump's friend Steve Bannon has said that his media outlet, Brietbert News is "the platform for the alt-right."

Although they both came from drastically different backgrounds, both men gained power among those who felt they had been disfranchised or otherwise overlooked by their country's leadership. In Germany it was the DAP and NSDAP who sought to draw working men away from communism and into a form of nationalism. They were anti-business, anti-bourgeois, and anti-capitalist. Trump, coming from a wealthy and capitalist background ran on the platform of anti-free trade, and pro working class. These similarities and differences will be examined to see just how different their leadership styles were, if at all.

Making it a reality

During a DAP meeting, Hitler met Dietrich Eckart, one of the founder's and a member of the Thule Society, an occult group based in Munich. The membership of the Thule Society read like a who's who of early Nazi organizers and those who lead Munich directly after World War I. Eckart would be Hitler's mentor and assist in making inroads for Hitler among the leaders of Germany. During this time, the DAP also in attempts to gain more members changed its name to the National Socialist German Worker's Party(NSDAP), commonly known as the Nazi Party.

The party's banner and the lasting symbol for not only the Nazi Party but for anti-semetic to this day was a red flag with a white swastika in the middle, created by Hitler as part of the reorganization.

After being discharged in 1920 Hitler began to work for the NSDAP full time and was known for his speeches. Although there was already some anti-marxist and a desire to undermine the existing Weimar Republic, Hitler was able to bring all the groups together under one common goal. Already known for his ability for polemic, rowdy speeches, in February 1921 Hitler spoke to over 6,000 people. Most of his speeches touched on the same ideas. He was against the treaty of Versailles, spoke ill of political rivals, and expanded on his belief that Marxists and Jews were the downfall of the German empire.

Hitler was a political tactician and so when many of the NSDAP formed a coup and wanted to join the rival German Socialist Party(DSP) Hitler left the party. He then came to them with what may be perceived as a peace offering, although it was nothing of the sort. Hitler stated that he would rejoin if, and only if the current chairman was removed and if the party headquarters stayed in Munich. Fearing what would happen if they did not allow Hitler to rejoin, the committee agreed.

Although they allowed him back in, there was still some push back regarding his message and his intended actions. The opponents even created fliers calling Hitler a traitor to not only the NSDAP but to the German people as a whole. Hitler pretending to be on the defensive began holding gatherings at beer houses where he spoke on how he was being railroaded and none of it was true. With his excellent oratorical skills, it was no wonder that on July 29th a special party congress convened and replaced Drexler with Hitler with only one out of 534 voting against him. Hitler now had complete control not only over the party, but the majority of the party members.

It took Hitler years to get to the position that he could influence substantial change for Germany as a country. Like Hitler, Trump began putting out feelers years before he ultimately was elected. As previously discussed, Trump became interested in politics around 2000. He eventually dropped out of the race, but for the next 15 years he toyed with varying levels of government. It wasn't until 2015 that he officially filed for the 2016 presidential race.

While many were surprised and pessimistic about his chances, he ran on a platform that spoke to many Americans. By 2016 The United States had seen an uptick in social, business, and immigration issues due to a variety of reasons. Some blamed the outgoing president for not stepping in, others blamed the entirety of the federal government for their archaic laws and tax codes. There was a lot of strife and instability in the years of 2014 through 2016. A small but vocal percent of the population was adamant that the reason behind all of these issues were illegal, and at times legal immigrants taking all the jobs. Between that and the fact that most industrial jobs were moving to Asia, it was the perfect time for someone to swoop in and pander.

A strong leader was needed, especially one that could heal a divided country. With war having been a constant backdrop for 14 years, and the gap between the wealthy and the poor ever widening, a white male who played upon the American Dream easily gained popularity and the republican nomination. There were those who worried about the rhetoric that he was using to gain supporters, many ignored him. They believed that without a doubt the Democratic nominee would win.

He likely would have lost if it not had been for the Democratic party not nominating Bernie Sanders, a very popular candidate to those who were liberal and wanted change, but not the change that Hillary Clinton could provide. The second main issue was that Hillary Clinton had skeletons in her closet, and when the media and the GOP discovered the skeletons, it was hard to divert the accusations and promises coming from the GOP.

During the 6 months leading up to the election, the media were beside themselves with what Trump was saying. They could not believe he was running on the falsehoods and hyperbole that he was. It seemed like every day news channels such as CNN and Fox were either supporting him, or trying to figure out how he could actually accomplish all the things that he was promising. Obviously, there were stations that were primarily against him, more liberal in nature such as CNN, Washington Post, and the New York Times. Then there were the news outlets that were conservative such as Fox News and Breitbert News.

He ran on a few specific promises that his supporters most wanted to hear. He promised to remove the Affordable Care Act, known as Obamacare, even though some of his supporters were actual recipients. He said that he would not repeal the whole thing, but would leave things such as preexisting conditions and help for college age children.

He said that he would stop the illegal immigration from Mexico by building a wall and having Mexico pay for it. He never talked about how or why this would happen, but Mexico was going to pay for it. His speeches were filled with people who screamed "make them pay" and supporters truly believed that this man could make another country pay for a massive and expensive wall separating the southwest United States from Mexico.

The one promise that really sold his supporters was "draining the swamp." He believed as many that politicians were in it only for themselves and never looked after the little guy. The belief was they created laws and regulations that only benefited them and their friends, while the middle class were suffering. Trump, not unlike Hitler saw this weakness and jumped on it. The people wanted someone to blame, and Trump gave it to them.

Another promise that resonated with the voters was to ban Muslims from coming into our country. Although FDR had said "The only think to fear is fear itself." That was ignored when Trump began to speak about how dangerous any and all Muslims were, harkening back to terrorist events, such as 9/11 and the Orlando dance club attack.

Trump laid out exactly how he was going to bring back manufacturing jobs to help those needing what they believed would be high wage, low tech jobs. On Jan 28 2016, Trump started with how he "was going to be the greatest jobs president God ever created."[25] He then went on to talk about how the United States would leave the Trans-Pacific Partnership and that he would personally renegotiate the North American Free Trade Agreement. He spoke directly to those who dislike the government by stating that he would use every lawful power to remedy trade disputes, including the application of tariffs.

Since the 1940s the United States has constantly been losing manufacturing jobs. According to experts there have been more than four million jobs lost with the increase in robotic technology and the steady move to countries that have a lower wage laws, and more individuals who are willing to work for those low wages.

To spark more outrage, and therefore more support, Trump yelled that he would impose stiff penalties on goods coming from China and Mexico, as those were the countries that many saw as the job takers. While he is within that right to impose tariffs on those countries that violate trade agreements, imposing additional or increased tariffs because he 'can' could lead to trade wars, and overall a much higher cost for goods bought.

The last two that are very important to his supporters were the cutting of taxes, and attacking ISIS once and for all. Trump promised that he and his administration would cut taxes across the board. Few, if any of his supporters looked at the cuts, which did in fact give tax cuts, but the top .01 percent, that he is part of would receive more tax benefits than the bottom 60 percent of the United States population. Obviously, his supporters were part of all socioeconomic classes, but a large part were those who were the working poor or middle class and all the saw was less taxes.

---

[25]Trump, Donald J. "Declaring American Economic Independence." June 28, 2016. Found at http://bit.ly/29blxEw.

ISIS is a fundamental threat to not only national security, but the security and safety of the entire world. They will attack Islamic and non-Islamic locations in hopes of increasing their military. Trump's campaign promise was that we, the United States would actively take away their oil fields and therefore start to squeeze them until there are no more. Everyone loved that idea, without realizing that the United States has had control over many of their oil supplies and that if we were to indeed take their "oil" it would require the United States to invade Saudi Arabia and maintain a large contingent of US soldiers to ensure the oil and gas would remain in the United States's control. When asked how those missions would be funded, he stated that it would be through the sale of controlled oil.

As can be seen Trump promised the world to those individuals who were plain sick and tired of being on the proverbial bottom. He spoke to the population who had seen or read about when the United States was great, and wanted to get back there. They wanted a piece of the American pie, and were tired of those they perceived as taking it from them. He specifically spoke to those who were part of the Tea Party and Alt-right movements who was sure that President Obama, being black, was the downfall of the United States and only when a white male again gained power would the United States be great again. Trump, seemingly oblivious to this portion of his supporters continued on, increasing the distance between his supporters and those of different political affiliations.

Unbelieved by the media and even many Republicans, Trump won the electoral college by 30 votes, but lost the popular vote by over 3 million. This set the stage for Trump to not only be elected as the President, but to ensure that his campaign promises were met, which is what is a leading contributor for the creation of this book.

What Trump did was extraordinary, he broke the stranglehold of Politicians as Presidents. But was it the right choice for the nation and for him? Will his business-like tendencies overrule the protection of the weaker citizens? Surely there are people everywhere, likely from both sides of the political fence that are creating memes and images now of Trump as Hitler. How much like Hitler is Trump? Is he bringing upon the fourth Reich, this time just with a different enemy? As comparisons are made, it will be up to you, the reader, to determine if enough evidence exists for the comparison to be made, or if it all boils down to an unneeded worry.

True Believers

This first thing that both Hitler and Trump had to do was get a group of people who truly and unwaveringly believed in what they were being told. Without that neither men would have reached the leadership roles they achieved. For Hitler, it was the industrial workers who worked for large companies. Be it communist companies, Jewish ran companies, or any company who did not firmly believe what Hitler spoke on. A German historian calls Hitler a "feel good dictator." Which I think aptly fits. He made the Germans feel good, and made sure that they believed he was taking care of them.

How did he make them feel that way? First, he gave them huge tax breaks and introduced social programs that benefitted everyone. He ensured that even during warfare no German went hungry. Hitler found out what the prevailing wage in The United States and Britain following World One I, and made sure that he paid more than double that to the German soldiers and their families. As before and during the war, people went hungry and taxes were constantly rising to pay for the war. Many citizens were so happy that they did not pay attention to the other, much darker side of Hitler's regime. In fact few, if any even questioned where the money came from to support the German populace. We now know that it came from plundering allies, laborers, Jews, and conquered lands.

Trump comparatively also had to establish a base supporter and after 15 years at war, and the economy sagging, it was not difficult to see how he would approach them. Being what could be considered a very good businessman, Trump like Hitler was very good at public speaking. Although Trump has more avenues for visibility with the advent of the internet and such, he also had to tread carefully. Voters in the US are more likely to vote their party than the opponent, but Trump knew that one large mistake and he could lose them before he securely had them. He also knew that his supporters once he had them, were not going to leave. Following the election, Trump went on a thank you tour and on January 23 he spoke in Iowa during which he said "I could stand in the middle of 5th avenue and shoot somebody and I wouldn't lose voters...It's like incredible."[26] This aligns with his belief that his people are the best people as opposed to opponent's supporters.

When Trump declared, he knew that he likely could not beat Hillary Clinton for the Democratic nomination, so he went against sage politicians for the Republican nominee. There are those who do not believe that he meant to win the election, but wanted to be the fly in the ointment for both political parties. Regardless if that is what happened or not, Trump went after those who see themselves are true patriots and were unhappy with the current establishment. His promises of increased jobs, lower taxes, and decreased immigration played on many people's emotions.

Another thing that Trump did from the very beginning was to portray himself as an American who never lies like those Washington politicians, that works hard to create jobs, and that truly cares about the American people. He portrayed many of his opponents as disloyal, uncaring, wealthy autocrats who like the status quo, and will not work with the people to fix things. His lack of what could be perceived as political correctness really spoke to people who believed the United States was moving away from the amendments and trying to be something we're not.

---

[26] Reilly, Katie. "Donald trump says he 'could shoot somebody' and not lose voters." Jan 23, 2016. Found at http://ti.me/1QlAcI2

It worked, and people flocked to hear Trump speak at rallies around the United States. He was not political, and spoke his mind about not only his opponents but about everything, especially about how he was going to help the little guy. As he is a great public speaker, he not only said what people wanted to hear, but he spoke about things they should be concerned with. From politicians wanting to take their weapons, to dismantling freedom of speech, to the fear that any day the United States could be attacked. This rhetoric really drew in those who believed they were outsiders like himself, someone who finally understood their needs and desires, and that he would help them.

This can be seen on a USAToday special on individuals who support Trump for President.[27] Many of those interviewed believed in the same lines of thinking. The same things that he had again and again voiced during commercials and rallies. That he was a man of the people, he would help the people instead of sitting in an ivory castle. He was not a politician and therefore he would owe nothing to anyone after the election, under a perceived notion that all politicians are bought and paid for. A notion that he himself vocalized.

Additional reasons where that he wasn't like Hillary who was a liar and just another piece in the puzzle. The desire to close our borders completely and make it about US first. Even though he has shown that many of these things are either not possible or he himself does not obey, that didn't stop people from only believing his word above all else. The one main thing that he voiced over and over was that he would bring this country back together through the creation of jobs, and by increasing our economy to the point where the racial and political divides were no longer visible.

---

[27] "Trump Nation" interactive by USAToday. Found at http://usat.ly/2kgIw1c

Hitler could cause a rally to explode in emotions and feelings towards those he opposed. He was very good at pulling the strings and understanding how his supporters felt and what they needed to hear. Like Hitler, Trump played on his supporter's desires and knew what to say to create a frenzy. The two important things that Trump hit on that his supporters loved and feared was that the entire election was rigged and it was the dishonest media doing it. This planted small seeds of contention that the US is still dealing with, months after the election.

Trump tiptoed around the issue of inciting violence against his opponents. At rallies, he came very close to turning his supporters against those of his opponents. Other times he was flat out telling his supporters that they should watch polling placed to ensure no corruption happened. He also asked on October 3, 2016 that his, supporters "scare" minority voters away from the polls.[28] Historically minority voters supported the democratic nominee and Trump knew that. After the election, he acknowledged that his supporters were violent and vicious before November, but should be more mellow and calm now that they won.

Both Trump and Hitler used their ability to command an audience to become base and vocal supporters of theirs. By preying on the weaknesses or insecurities that citizens had in troubling times, both men were able to achieve political clout and the people behind them to reach their ultimate goal. For Hitler that was to become the leader of Germany, and for Trump it was to become the President of the United States of America. They both achieved this goal primarily through large speaking engagements and dedicated and vocal supporters.

---

[28] Stern, George. "Trump facing lawsuit after calling for fans to scare people away from polls." October 3, 2016. found at http://bit.ly/2kkyVXh

Power Play

Neither Trump nor Hitler received their political positions freely and without strife. Both men had to politically maneuver to gain their desired positions. This has happened in the United States a hand full of times. John Quincy Adams, Rutherford B. Hayes, Benjamin Harrison historically received the electoral vote but lost the popular decision. Recently President G.W. Bush lost the popular vote to Al Gore, but still became President.

Hitler manipulated the NSDAP to oust the former leader and put him in charge. Then through the election process in 1922, he assisted in placing NSDAP members in prominent government positions therefore opening the door for the actions of 1923. After the Reichstag fire, Hitler saw his chance to come to the assistance of the current leadership. Once he had done that he moved to be brought in as a Chancellor. Since NSDAP members occupied many of the voting chairs, and with public support, Hitler was able to take over command of Germany and declare himself Fuhrer of Germany.

Trump likewise was able to insert himself in the early stages of the 2016 presidential election cycle. Likely due to his business skills, he was able to discern what the people wanted to hear and he gave it to them. He came in as the underdog that was not like those nasty politicians. With the stagnation of the government in previous years, the people wanted something new and different. Obviously, he did not mention that much of the stagnation was due to his own party not willing to work with the democratic president. By glossing over that, all they saw was an ineffective president and house leadership.

When allegations started to surface against Clinton, he knew that it was the perfect time to strike with talks of political corruption, and with the possibility of a rigged election. As many of his supporters were already disillusioned, this spoke to them in ways that another politician would not have been able to. He was the outsider, and he was going to save the United States. His tempo and tone really set the mood for the election and he was able to easily win the nomination.

The Presidential election was going to be more difficult, but he counted on a strong 3rd party candidate to take some votes away from Clinton. Even though he upped his rhetoric, the night of the election was close. In the end, Trump had won the electoral votes, but had lost the popular vote. Since the electoral votes are what counts, he was elected. However, still to this day he is unable to believe that he did not win the election. This could be his ego being bruised, but by planting that seed of doubt during the primaries his supporters bought into it. His claim is that three million illegal immigrants voted against him. There is no evidence, and when media displays the lack of evidence or asks for additional information, he hedges, or call them fake news in order to ignore them. Many of his supporters to this day believe that anywhere between 3 to 5 million votes were illegally cast, with every single one being for Clinton.

On January 24, 2017, more than two months after his victory, Sean Spicer the press secretary reiterated that "The President does believe that [illegal votes were cast], I think he's stated that before and stated his concern of voter fraud and people voting illegally during the campaign and continues to maintain that belief based on studies and evidence people have brought to him." However, when pushed, Spicer cannot list who or what has provided the voting statistics. To date, even though people are calling for a comprehensive look at voter fraud, and if there were more than 3 million illegally cast ballots, it should be looked into, Spicer and Trump reply with "Maybe we will look into it."

The claims are that 14% of those who voted were illegally voting. This number is backed up by a study in 2008 that stated that up to 14% of those surveyed stated they were illegally registered to vote. However, the authors of the studies claimed that less than half claimed to have voted, and in 2010 that number had dropped to 2.2%. The Brennan Center for Justice wrote a report titled "The Truth about Voter Fraud" and found that between .00004% and .00009% of those registered to vote were illegally doing so.[29] Of the 126 million votes that were cast, that would mean between 5,040 and 11,340 were illegal. That is a far cry from the 3-5 million he claims.

Even while preparing to meet the Japanese Prime Minister; Trump, his advisor Stephen Miller, and Sean Spicer continued to press the point about how Trump should have won New Hampshire. Their believe was if it had not been for the bus loads of individuals who voted there illegally. During what was supposed to be a meeting to discuss his Supreme Court nominee, he instead bemoaned on how he would have won. It has been three weeks since Trump was inaugurated President, yet he is continuing to press the issue regarding voter fraud, with no evidence, and no intent of an investigation.

New Hampshire however, has spoken out on the claims. Brian Buonamano, an assistant attorney general, has confirmed that the general election was relatively normal in percentage of voters, and therefore does not indicate some conspiracy to rob Trump of a victory, as he was elected President. Why is he so pre-occupied with what will likely amount of a complete fallacy?

---

[29] Liptak, Kevin and Dan Merica. "Trump believes millions voted illegally, WH says – but provides no proof." CNN found at http://cnn.it/2kffDmt

Could it be that republican politicians in New Hampshire and other localities are using his belief of voter fraud to pass measures that would make it more difficult for certain segments of the population. In New Hampshire alone, the Republican legislation has proposed 10 such measures.

Not unlike Hitler, Trump has delusions of grandeur and cannot believe why someone may not like him. That is directly seen in the fact that he cannot stop talking about how he won the election both electorally and popularly. This ego was what lost Hitler World War II, and has already caused some supporters of Trump's to distance themselves. They wanted a man to fight for them, not someone who is continuing to repeat what is likely a lie. Those that are part of "Trump Nation" or the diehard, loyal fans have no problem repeating his lies and using the illegal voting speech as a reason Trump deserves to be President.

Media

Even though the media was not as prevalent as it is now, both Hitler and Trump depended on sympathetic news outlets to not only support their propaganda and ideals, but to quash anything that may be true, but negative. Especially now, media can make you or they can break you, and Trump knows that especially with his background in a media driven industry. While Hitler did not have the experience, his associates were ready and willing to roll out the propaganda machine.

Once in power, Hitler called on Joseph Goebbels to become his minister of propaganda. Goebbels had been drawn to the NSDAP following Hitler's release from prison. Initially he worked for other Nazi Party leaders on weekly newspapers and doing small administrative tasks. Soon he became the party speaker and the representative of another Nazi party branch. After some political infighting, Hitler reached out to Goebbels and offered him a proverbial olive branch. Goebbels, having been initially turned off by Hitler became enamored with him after a beer hall rally. From that day forward, Goebbels swore his alliance and total loyalty.

As they began to work together, Goebbels continued to be impressed with Hitler, and even wrote in his journal that "I love him … He has thought through everything." Soon Goebbels began to adapt his political ideas to that of Hitler. He was considered an important individual in Hitler's life and was given great responsibility leading up the Hitler's appointment to Chancellor.

Eventually he was given the position of Ministry of Propaganda and he, with his previous experience, jumped at the chance to control not only written media, but radio and the newly developed live action video.

Nothing was released to the press without a Goebbel spin on it. It helped Hitler immensely that Goebbels not only believed in Hitler's image, but had the speaking ability to ensure things ran smoothly. He was able to convince even the strongest opponents that Hitler's ideas were strong and should be carried out. This was especially true on his publication of anti-Semitic fliers and radio broadcasts. He was seen as part of the benevolent Nazi Party that cared about the workers and really wanted a better Germany. For those individuals who only had radios or newspapers, all they knew was the wonderful things that Hitler was doing by way of Goebbels.

This attitude and behavior can be seen currently in the form of Sean Spicer, the Press Secretary for President Trump. He is unable to control as much as Goebbels could, simply due to the ease of media access. What he has that Hitler didn't was an already established position that media sources go to for information from the White House. This places him in a very secure spot to dictate however they see fit. Trump also assisted him in the 18 months leading up to the election by hinting at dishonesty among media sources.

As mentioned briefly before, during the initial rallies and campaign functions Trump began his undermining of the media. In this day and age, everyone has the internet, and with bloggers, journalists, and the public being able to write and publish something on their cell phones it could turn ugly fast. Trump knew that things happened quickly and to stay above the curve you had to be proactive and provocative. His persona was already provocative and many knew him from his days as being a reality show personality. To be proactive, he used Twitter constantly and was always talking about something or someone. This kept his face in the news and allowed him to direct how people saw him.

Before a discussion on Trumps essential war on the media, one thing should be known. Although there has been media bias since there has been media, the amount of bias has escalated in the last decade. With higher visibility on websites like Facebook and Twitter, anyone can create a website and discuss whatever they want. What this has done is create fringe "news outlets" that are really nothing more than one or more frustrated individuals who believe that everything is the fault of the illuminati. Obviously, there are levels of bias, and the closer to the center an outlet is, the more balanced the reporting will be.

With media bias comes the additional fact that in the span of 10 minutes, someone can write up a piece of "news" and publish it on their website. All it takes is one person to see it and share it on a social media site, and their opinions and frustrations will be seen by those who feel similarly. Instead of having groups that meet and talk about conspiracies or threats, now one can connect with people across the globe that feel the same way. While it has been enlightening for many, there is also a dark side where people with ill intentions can now communicate with others, thereby validating their beliefs. Validation leads to the creation of a website, which leads to "news outlets" that are full of poor research if at all. Most of the articles are also unsubstantiated drivel that someone believes is true.

One of the first instances was during a press conference where Trump said

> "So they [the media] criticize me for being too tough the first day. The second day they said, 'Donald Trump's not as tough as we thought,' can you believe it?

You can't win with these people. Look at all these cameras zooming. They are the most dishonest people in the world. The media. They are the worst. They are very dishonest people. They are terrible.

Honestly, and I don't mean all, but I mean like 75, 80 percent. And they know it, they know. These are not stupid people, but they're very dishonest people, in many cases."[30]

To prove his point even more he got the crowd involved, he made sure to whip them into a frenzy with his remarks and then ask if they trusted the media. Of course, the response was a resounding no. So, what brought on this diatribe regarding the media? During the first presidential debate Megyn Kelly and Fox news asked him tough questions that he was not prepared for.

Obviously, the media helped him win not only the nomination but also the election by ensuring that they filmed everything. He was akin to an actor and the media was having a field day with it. This just increased when he began to incite his rallies with talks of a wall and having Clinton imprisoned. Some experts believe that if it was not for media camps on both sides of the political fence fawning/fighting over him, his campaign would have fizzled early. What is done is done, and the only thing now is to make sure that the news is reported on. Sort of.

Since that talk in April 2016, Trump has continued the rhetoric that the media is out to get him. He believes in a captive press, one that adores him and gives him plenty of attention. The only issue is that while they have given him plenty of attention,

---

[30] Irvine, Don. "Donald Trump Calls the Media "dishonest;" Gives them Credit for Helping His Campaign." April 2016. Found at http://bit.ly/2kqnWOr

much of it has been negative. He could not stand by while his name was drug through the mud when they reported on something he said. Yes, as anyone who has watched more than 10 minutes of news in the last 12 months, even those things that he spoke that were then replayed are wrong. May 2016, he tweeted to "Not believe the biased and phony media quoting people who work for my campaign."

Many news outlets reported tantrums during the campaign cycle as fodder to rile up base supporters. However, his attacks on the media has increased, with emphasis on how he has been mistreated. In line with his belief that the election was rigged, he jumped at newscasters with giving him a faulty mic, fact checking his answers, you name it, if it made him look bad, it was fake, dishonest, and biased.

Even though leading up to the election according to Washington Post's Paul Farhi, Trump had a total of 822 minutes of screen time, compared to that of Clinton who had 386 minutes, 90 minutes of that being about her email servers. Initially he wanted it to be like back in the 70s, 80s, and early 90s when he called a station and they would drop everything to talk to him. But this isn't the same media, and he is not the same Trump. Trump is used to the media waiting on his phone call, and fawning on his every word. This election the media did not so they, they held him to task. It is unlikely he understands why this change occurred, and ensures there is constant interaction, even if just by a response to his social media posts. In fact, the media was so horrible that he began stating that "If you don't know me, then you shouldn't write about me, you don't know what I am like." This is a falsehood that almost everyone knows. You don't have to know a journalist by name for them to write about you. There are too many articles and too short of time for every journalist to personally meet the individual and form a relationship before writing an article.

As his outrage at the media increased, he hinted that he would loosen the libel laws and sue the journalists for libel. He said that the next time a news outlet wrote a "hit piece" he would sue them and win money instead of them being protected. His anti-media campaign went after the more liberal media outlets like the Washington Post, CNN, and the New York Times. Even now, two months after being elected, he is continuing to tweet about how wrong they are. As this tweet shows, he even went so far as to imply that someone that agrees with him should buy the "failing" New York Times. After this tweet was published, New York Times came back and said that their subscriber list is increasing and that they are not failing.

On the topic of Twitter, Donald Trump uses twitter a lot, and most of it is to slander, yell at, or call liberals losers, and to pretty much talk about whatever he is upset about. Anytime anything does not go his way, or he does not perceive it as going his way he gets upset and starts to yell on Twitter. For example, recently many reports have come out that say his approval rating is low, one of the lowest for an incoming president. In addition, polls were taken regarding his recent and very controversial "travel ban". This was his response:

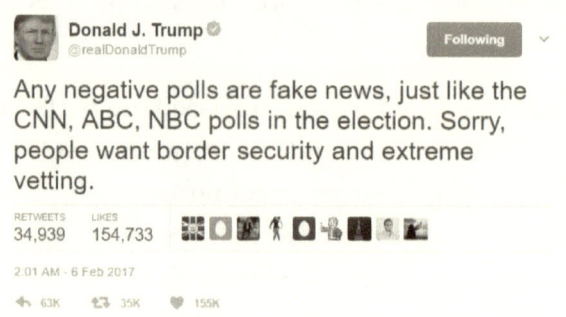

Many who see these posts laugh at the stupidity of them and go about their day. The problem is that these tweets are indicative of his instability and poses a serious risk to national security. He will and does talk about many things, mostly benign grievances that he has with union leaders, democrats, and people who don't agree with him. There have been however some tweets that when looked at objectively could be dangerous such as lying about terrorist attacks and threatening countries such as Iran.

The issue is that there are those who have supported him, or are trying to give him a chance now that he is president who think that this kind of attitude, and condemnation of media is okay. The United States thrives on an open media, and with tweets about how dishonest they are, it can discredit them. This is the first step in taking control over media access.

The second step is something that Trump has already done. Because of his issues with the media, and the fact he likely does not have time to speak with the media he enlisted a spin doctor, Kellyanne Conway to take some of the media heat off of him. In the end this may actually be part of Trump's undoing, but currently she is creating enough press herself to keep some attention off of Trump's actions.

Conway is also very active on twitter and while she is not as negative and defensive, she does fire back at individuals who she feels have slighted her or Trump. This creates a cycle that has seen an unprecedented attack on the media. From her saying that the media and the president should be "co-parents" of the government, and how they may need to "renegotiate their relationship," to saying that what the Press Secretary and the President do is give "alternative facts." Yes, you heard that right, Conway, supposedly a very smart woman, told the media that they will lie to them.

Due to the recent court decision against the administration on the immigration ban, Stephen Miller has also actively engaged the media. The one main topic that Miller is discussing is the decision. His main goal is to undermine the public's confidence with the judicial system. Miller believes as Trump does that a judge in Washington should not be able to make a decision that affects the entire nation. When the three-person 9th court of appeals upheld the ban unanimously, he countered with how they have a "history of overreaching" and that their decision as a "judicial usurpation of the power." It does not seem to matter to Miller that multiple courts ruled against the "ban."[31]

This attempt to undermine the judicial system is worrying because the United States is based on a three-part system that allows for a balance of power. The judicial branch ensures that the laws created by the Legislative Branch, and enforced by the Executive Branch are in line with the constitution and are lawful. The Judicial Branch is not only the nine-member Supreme Court, but also lower courts that are at the state level and hear cases regarding federal issues.

Couple that with Spicer and Trump threatening to remove certain media stations from the press conferences and you have a perfect storm of media restriction and propaganda creation. Obviously from the fact that Trump is still talking about how the TV stations lied about how many people were at the inauguration, to his utter disbelief that media would say he is lying. All three of these individuals are slowly twisting the truth to where now when you are talking to someone and you say "I read this on CNN/MSNBC/Etc." the response you get is "Fake news" and they will just stop listening. Of all the things that Trump has done that compares to Hitler, this right here is the closest and most significant.

Many people think that in 4 or 8 years' things will go back to the way they were with the media. Especially how the media is supposed to be a steward over the president, to ensure that the administration is being held accountable for their actions. The issue with that, and some historians and political scientists can tell you, is Trump, Conway, and Spicer are creating an atmosphere that will take decades if not longer to return to pre-2015

---

[31] Fang, Marina. "Trump Adviser Stephen Miller disastrously tries to defend Trump." February 12, 2017. Found at http://huff.to/2kX9goG

standards. The main reason is that now the media is not trusted. While before those same people who create conspiracy theory websites from their basements didn't trust the media, now it is main stream. Smart individuals who used to think critically and process before making a decision are now not believing anything except from certain media sources.

It has become apparent that Trump only trusts specific news outlets such Breitbart, so much that he fought a Fox News journalist over the validity of a statement by holding up a printed copy of a Breitbart article. Trump has also reportedly saved a seat in the front row of the White House Press room for a Breitbart reporter. In a joint press conference with Canadian Prime Minister Justin Trudeau that occurred on February 13, 2017 Trump only answered four questions, and the two outlets that were chosen to ask them were the conservative Daily Caller and the ABC Affiliate in Washington D.C.. Even though a major development regarding Secretary of National Security, Mike Flynn had occurred prior to the conference, neither outlet asked about it. Some wonder if this had been prearranged, even after both reporters stated that they did not speak with the White House prior to asking their question.[32]

When the "adversary" media is removed, there is no one to hold the President or others in the administration accountable for their actions. Many think of the media as a fourth branch, one to overlook and to bring them to task. Without that open and free media, the ability to remove or add policies without rebuke will exist. Even with the media present, there has been things that occurred that even the administration was not prepared to be called on. Like with Hitler's Germany, having control over the

---

[32] Borchers, Callum, "Here's how Trump avoided questions about Michael Flynn in today's press conference." February 13, 2017. Found at http://wapo.st/2lJ9xe8

media allowed civil liberties and censorship to reign supreme. We have already started to see some of both occur, but how long can the free media keep going before they are completely closed from press releases and meetings? The Trump administration has already looked at the whistleblower act which may curtail many of the anonymous reports. How soon will major outlets be limited to gathering their news from "approved" media outlets?

Civil Liberties

One of the first actions that an incoming leader does to ensure the start of complete control is the decrease or total removal of civil liberties. The path usually begins with an event that the leader can twist and use as propaganda in order to curtail the rights and liberties of their citizens. This isn't exclusive to dictators, or fascist leaders, but to many who have a hidden agenda.

Hitler used the Reichstag fire on February 27, 1933 to begin his removal of liberties. The arsonist was believed to be a young Dutch unemployed bricklayer who was part of the communist party. Less than a month earlier Hitler had been appointed as the Chancellor of Germany. Following the fire, he immediately urged the then President Paul von Hindenburg to pass an emergency decree to counter what was perceived as the ruthless confrontation of the Communist Party of Germany. To this day there are some who believe that the Nazi party helped to orchestrate the event as a false flag event.

False flags are events that are designed to deceive outsiders in such a way that they believe an entity, group, or nation was responsible, while another was responsible. If the Reichstag fire was a false flag for instance, the Nazi party was actually responsible, but placed the blame on the Communist Party. One way that this occurs is if the Nazi party found a young, unemployed member of the communist party and pays him a large sum of money or ensures his family will be taken care of in the future. This way when the fire took place, the Nazi party could "rightfully" claim that the fire was done by a communist. Conspiracy theorists are usually the only ones to believe in false flags. This decreases the probability of the real culprit will be discovered. Due to the event involved, there is usually no witnesses or proof to blame another.

False flag or not, with the Reichstag fire and the decree issued by Hitler, the Nazi party had the legal right to arrest Germans who were part of the Communist party, including individuals of the government. This then forced an election in which the Nazi party produced propaganda stating that Germany was on the brink of a communist revolution and by conjuring the Reichstag fire. The election gave many seats to the Nazi Party, but there was still 17% that were communist. Hitler's plan was to outlaw the communists from being part of the parliament on grounds of possible corruption. This this allowed the Nazi party to fill empty parliament seats with fellow Nazi party members.

Hitler needed 2/3rds of the seats to be on his side for the Enabling Act to commence. This act states that the Chancellor is given the power to pass laws by decree, thereby not requiring majority votes from the parliament. At that point the parliamentary went from a plurality party to a majority, allowing Hitler to further consolidate his power. On March 23, 1933, the enabling act vote passed and was supported by not only the Nazi Party, but the Centre Party, and many smaller middle-class parties. When it enacted on March 27, 1933, Hitler effectively became the dictator of Germany.

Following the decree and the enabling act, Hitler ordered the construction of Dachau, the first of many concentration and deaths camps created under the Nazi Party. When it certain that the Nazi Party had complete control, Hitler began to create special courts that were led by Nazi sympathizers to punish those who were political opponents. It was not long before those found guilty were sent to Dachau by Hitler's personal military the SA "Stormtroopers." The SA did the bidding of both Hitler and the

Nazi Party with less regard for German laws. Hitler used these men to enact martial law and to ensure curfews were abided by.

Other important events that occurred in 1933 that set the tempo for the majority of Hitler's tenue in power was the civil laws passed that barred Jews from holding positions in civil service, in legal and medical professions, and in teaching and university professions. He ensured that those of Jewish ancestry were cast out from the community as much as possible. During speeches and with fliers, the Nazi party would encourage the boycotting and destruction of Jewish-owned shops and businesses.

It wasn't just individuals that Hitler was concerned with. To have complete and utter control over the German population, the Nazi Party began burning books created by not only Jews but also any not approved by the Reich. While this does not seem in our modern day open society something that could happen, look at how Trump is marginalizing media outlets? Now imagine that the existing platforms for dissension were already removed by Goebbel's control of newsprint and radio. The only way that a German citizen could be exposed to dissenting ideas and arguments were by book. With control over books and other printed material, there was little that could reach media consumers that Goebbels and the Nazi Party did not control.

The persecution of Jews really began when in 1935 Hitler and the Nazi party deprived Jews of their German citizenship and other basic rights. In 1936 Germany hosted the Olympic games to show to the world that they were accepting of all faiths and nationalities, they removed the signs barring Jews until after the games were over. Following that Jews lost the right to vote. Then in 1936, Germany annexed Austria as part of the German Nation and Kristallnacht occurred which resulted in more than 30,000

Jews arrested in both Germany and Austria. With complete power, the Nazi Party began to require Jews to carry identification cards with a J on them, as well as not being able to attend events, such as concerts. When that wasn't enough, all Jewish children had to go to Jewish only schools, sell their businesses and provide the SA with all securities and jewels they had. The last step was to ensure that all Jews obeyed curfews that ensured they were all in certain places at certain times.

All of what Hitler did would not have been possible without the levels of censorship that both the Nazi Party and Germany as a whole commanded. When the only rhetoric you hear is what a group wants you to hear, you will eventually believe it. Goebbels is probably one of the best at twisting the truth to make it what the Nazi's wanted it to be. Without him, the completion of Hitler's plan may not have been fulfilled.

The United States has gone through similar periods of time when nationalities or races were persecuted for who they are. Native Americans were rounded up into reservations. Japanese Americans were removed from their communities, lost their businesses and houses while they were sent to live in "internment camps" and "relocation camps" which were intentionally named as to not be compared to the German "concentration camps."

Like with Germany the United States used a large-scale event to create regulations that allowed for civil rights to be bent or in some cases completely disregarded. The Japanese attack on Pearl Harbor on December 7, 1941 was just such an event. In response President Roosevelt signed Executive Order 9066 which allowed for the deportation and incarnation at the order of regional military commanders. The United States set up regions where the commanders could designate "military areas" where "any and all persons may be excluded." Eventually all Japanese Americans were excluded from the entire West Coast except for in the government's camp. By the end of the war, more than 130,000 mainland Japanese were either voluntary or forcibly put in the "internment camps." The United States government overreached by including those who had a minimum of 1/16th Japanese blood and even including orphan infants. It is unsure how the government felt that infants could be a national security threat.

Since World War II, there have been small events that allowed the President to create laws to ensure that the citizens were safe. Enacting curfews during and immediately following large natural disasters is a simple way to curtail civil liberties while maintaining public safety. Laws regarding ownership of weapons have also been enacted to increase public safety, even though some of those laws are not effective and they are not short term like curfew initiation. The most restrictive is for the President or other leader is to enact martial law, which states that all viable civil rights are on hold for the duration of the event. Although not used frequently, it is the one of the last options.

The United States has only enacted this law 11 times. The majority being natural disasters and events surrounding coal mines. The last time was in 1961 when the Governor of Alabama declared martial law against the freedom riders, a group of individuals who entered Alabama and who according to the governor "violated our laws and customs," which led to "outbreaks of lawlessness and mob action." Even the World Trade Center did not cause martial law to be enacted. Trump in the first month of being president, insinuated that if Chicago, with a large murder rate, did not get it under control, he would send in federal agents.

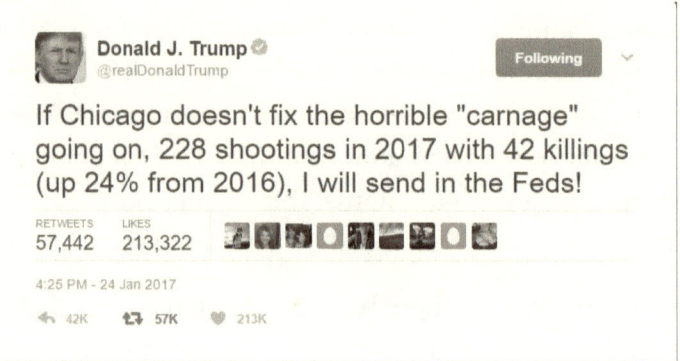

The only way that he could do this, as the 10th amendment states that the powers not delegated to the United States by the constitution, nor prohibited by it to the states, are reserved for the States respectively, or to the people. The Federal government cannot force state or local governments to act against their will. This is not the only time that the 10th amendment is pushed to the side by the Trump administration.

President Trump when inaugurated began a flurry of Executive Orders and Presidential memos that some could perceive as limiting civil rights. "Border Security and Immigration Enforcement Improvement," signed on January 25, allows for the hiring of thousands of Border patrol officers, while at the same time setting in motion steps to build a massive and expensive wall between the United States and Mexico. While the order is to decrease illegal immigration from Mexico into the United States. When you read closer however, there is a section that is important. Section 10, states that the federal government can empower state and local law enforcement officers to perform the functions of an immigration officer. This is worrying language because taken to the extremes it could be that legal citizens would be required to prove their citizenship.

On February 9, 2017 the first individual was deported under the new Executive Order. Guadalupe Garcia de Rayos, a mother of two children who are U.S. Citizens, was detained and deported following her yearly immigration check in. De Rayos came to the U.S. illegally in the mid-90s when she was 14 for a better life. In 2008 she was arrested following a workplace raid that discovered she had been using a false social security card. In 2009 she was convicted of felony criminal impersonation. She tried to voluntarily deport, but the court refused her request.

In 2013 she became the subject of a removal order, and was to report to the immigration office for routine check-ins. She did so for 7 years, always being sent back to her family, however this year, days after the Executive Order was issued, she was arrested and deported. Yes, she was a criminal, one that since her arrest has followed the law according to the US Immigration office that she reports to. So, while there are thousands of illegal alien criminals in United States jails, why was this woman, who had not been deported for the last four years, suddenly removed?[33] Was she a hardened criminal that was actively hurting United States citizens? No. She was by all accounts, a loving mother, whose children are now motherless, unless they decide to move to Mexico.

While this case shows the implementation of one Executive Order, and by the law, this was a clear-cut violation and therefore did result in deportation. However, when will a Hispanic U.S. Citizen be asked for papers just to prove they in fact belong here? Is there not more important stuff to do then enter US cities and cast a net, to see what may fall in? Apparently not, as at least six states around the United States were raided by Immigration and

---

[33] Shoichet, Catherine. "Immigrants and crime: Crunching the numbers." CNN Politics. Full article can be found at: http://cnn.it/1L7GVp2

Customs Enforcement (ICE) beginning February 6, 2017 and ending on February 10, 2017. This will not be an isolated incident as apparently, ICE is currently taking part in Operation Cross Check.[34]

The need to prove citizenship is becoming reality when a U.S. Citizen arriving from South America was detained at the airport. Sidd Bikkannavar, a US-born NASA employee was traveling back from Chili when he was detained by Customs and Border Patrol (CBP). CBP handed him a form that stated they could look at his cell phone. The issue was, the cell phone Bikkannavar was in possession of was a NASA provided phone with sensitive information on it. When he refused to provide the pin, they threatened to arrest him. Unsure as to what to do, he provided the pin number, and the CBP agent apparently took the phone for an extended amount of time. Upon receiving the phone back, Bikkannavar immediately returned to work and told his supervisors what had occurred. As CBP do not have blanket clearance, the information they retrieved off of his phone could have possible economic and security issues.[35] As this event just occurred there is not additional information regarding the incident.

If those orders were not enough, an additional order was signed. "Executive Order: Enhancing Public Safety in the Interior of the United States," strengthens the previous Executive Order and can further exacerbate civil rights issues. Trump and his administration has already talked about orders, or memos regarding rights for LGBTQIA+ individuals. Currently there are anti-discrimination laws protecting individuals, but with the

---

[34] US Government. "Operation Cross Check." More information regarding this and other homeland security plans can be found here: http://bit.ly/2lETYs3
[35] Croft, Jay. "US-Born NASA scientist says he was told to unlock his phone at the border." February 13, 2017. Found at http://cnn.it/2klWgMd

swipe of a pen, they can all be removed. While the federal government at this moment is not pushing through discrimination or other civil right removing legislation there are many states and municipalities that are.

Following the inauguration there were protests spanning the globe against Trump and everything that he stands for. Some of the protests became violent, others like the women's march the next day was peaceful and saw hundreds of thousands marching for women's rights. Since then multiple states have begun their legislative cycles with laws to remove certain rights given to them either by being human, or by the constitution.

Arkansas, West Virginia, Mississippi, Kansas, Louisiana, and Oklahoma have all proposed bills that would take the basic right of bodily independence from women. These bills set a dangerous precedent that a woman does not have control over her body. This equates a woman as less than a man, in some instances, their own body being controlled by a male spouse or relative. For a country that stands on individual rights, this undermines much of what a person is.

Arkansas has proposed House Bill 1032 which is "An Act to Create the Arkansas Unborn Child Protection From Dismemberment Abortion Act; and For Other Purposes." Initially the media declared this as a man could sue a doctor and/or the pregnant female if she decides to have an abortion. In response, many Arkansas politicians attempted to downplay the bill. With whatever spin they want to put on it, the truth is this is a ban on abortion following the end of the first trimester. There is no exception for rape or incest, and it allows her husband — if she has one — to sue her over the death of their child. Even if he rapes her, he can sue her.[36] If the woman is a minor, her parents can sue her. Boiling it down to the basic elements, this bill, which passed, says that a pregnant woman's body is not under her control, but under that of a male figure.

West Virginia, Kansas, and Louisiana all have very similar bills to Arkansas's newly passed law. The main different is theirs do not allow for suing the individual. Even still, court justices have worried about the impact on women's right to privacy. Oklahoma takes these bills one step further. On February 8, 2017 Oklahoma performed a first reading and tabled for discussion House Bill 1441.

This bill is like one that was struck down by the U.S. Supreme Court, but with a new administration, the hope is that if challenged the Court would find in the state's favor. This bill says that if a woman, an adult US citizen, wants to have an abortion, regardless of how far along, or by what circumstances must have a written letter allowing her to do so by the "father" of the fetus. Not only that, but the woman must tell the doctor the man's name. If after contacted, the man demands a paternity test, the woman cannot receive an abortion, which could result in the pregnancy progressing to the point where it is not legal in the state to have one.[37] Currently, both HB 1441 and HB 1549 — a bill that would block women from aborting a fetus if it has, or is suspected of having a genetic abnormality — are to be presented again on February 14, 2017.

Tennessee interestingly is not going for an abortion bill as such, but instead is repealing a state statute that assists couples

---

[36] Arkansas Government. "House Bill 1032." Passed January 27, 2017. Full bill at http://bit.ly/2l2NaBf

[37] State of Oklahoma, "House Bill 1441." First read February 8, 2017. Full bill can be found at: http://bit.ly/2lKO59p

who have surrogates or artificial insemination consider the child the legitimate child of a husband, or other partner.[38] What the legislator wanted to do was remove that legitimacy and therefore will remove the state from intruding into how a woman conceives her child. That isn't what the wording says though, and after a divorce case in October 2016, in which same-sex couples are afforded all of the rights and responsibilities of heterosexual couples, this bill seeks to force same-sex couples, and heterosexual couples who are unmarried to establish legitimacy in court, thereby affecting families financially.

This legislation does not end there however. Due to the extent of the protests that occurred directly following the inauguration, many state politicians worry that there may be negative impacts due to future protests. Not only do we have states trying to directly interfere with a woman's body, but now with a constitutional right. Five states have proposed legislation that curtails an American's right to peacefully gather as part of the 1st Amendment. They range from asinine to downright scary.

North Dakota introduced a bill that would allow motorists to run over and kill any protester obstructing a highway as long as the driver does so accidentally. Yes, North Dakota wants it to be okay if you "accidentally" run someone over. In Minnesota, they seek to stiffen fines for freeway protesters and would allow prosecutors to seek a full year of jail time for protesters blocking a highway. Iowa has promised to introduce a bill to crack down on highway protesters. Washington, and Seattle in particular are trying to get a law passed that reclassifies civil disobedience as a felony regarding "economic Terrorism". Finally, Michigan introduced and then shelved a law that would increase penalties

---

[38] State of Tennessee, "House Bill 1406." First read February 9, 2017. Full bill can be found at: http://bit.ly/2kFcU5z

against protestors and would make it easier for businesses to sue individual protesters for their actions, otherwise known as the "anti-picketing" law.[39]

One order that is part of strengthening our borders had an unintended civil rights consequence. On January 27, President Trump signed Executive Order: "Protecting the Nation from Foreign Terrorist Entry into the United States." This is important to nationalism and will be discussed in detail in the next chapter, but the important aspect for this conversation is that it allowed individuals from various countries that are primarily Muslim. Although the claim was that this was not a ban on Muslims, it is a ban, as the only countries affected are Muslim. What this allowed was for the US government along with Customs agents to stop individuals from these countries from entering into the United States. Normally that would not have raised such an issue, but the order also allowed for the holding of individuals who have legal visas or green cards.

In response to the ban not ban of Muslims, individuals began to protest airports. Due to the size of the protest, Portland International Airport, has deemed large protests inside the Terminal will not occur again. Representatives have said that they will allow a "protest zone" that will still allow individuals to engage the public, just not in the terminal. The issue with that is free speech, especially in Oregon is very coveted and the leader of the local resistance group says that they will protest where they want, and how they want, while still maintaining a peaceful

---

[39] Woodman, Spencer. "Republican lawmakers in five states propose bills to criminalize peaceful protest." January 19, 2017. Found at http://bit.ly/2iF8jDG

atmosphere. It will be interesting to see how the airport reacts if another protest occurs.[40]

After the protests on the ban were done, and judges from around the nation called a halt to the order, a young woman was held at the airport on her way to a convention in California. Ibtihaj Muhammad has an Arabic name and she wears the hijab. In fact, she is the first American to wear a hijab during the Olympics, where she not only represented the country and Islam with pride, but she came away with a bronze medal in fencing, which is normally not a sport that American's excel in. She was born and raised in New Jersey and has an American passport, but that did not stop customs from detaining her for two hours.[41] Was it due to the ban, or was it because by her wearing a hijab she was considering a possible enemy of the state? Her civil rights were violated by a law that was essentially designed to do just that.

Another way that we are seeing is the gradual and slow process of the 1st Amendments, freedom of speech and religion. Trump's administration does not believe in climate change, or the global warming affect. There are however, many who do believe that it is something that is occurring and could have drastic consequences on our lives. Some of those who believe work for the federal government. Some work for the national park system, others for NASA, NOAA, and many more. Since Trump does not believe it is real, he first told the employees to not talk about climate change at all, not to the media, not on twitter, nothing. Scientists do not go easy into that good night. They stood up and said no. Instead of shaking his head and trying to reason with

---

[40] Dooris, Pat. "PDX bans large protests in airport terminal." February 6, 2017. Found at http://bit.ly/2kpslP8

[41] Worley, Will. "US Olympic fencer Ibtihaj Muhammad says she was detained by customs after Donald Trump's 'Muslim Ban.'". February 9, 2017. Found at http://ind.pn/2lnkxlb.

them, he put a global gag order on federal twitter accounts and told them not to speak to the media.

What did they do? Did they close up shop and wait for his fit to be over? No, they created alternate twitter accounts. Badlands National Park because Badhombreslands. Soon other national parks and agencies joined in. In total as of Febuary 9, there were 64 rogue twitter feeds, not including the "RoguePOTUSstaff" which is said to be someone in the White House. A couple of them state they are in no way associated with the park, or agency. Most however, employees. Why? Because like Rogue FDA says; You can take our official twitter, but you'll never take our free time!

Rogue FDA
@rogueUSFDA

Follow

Can't wait for President Trump to call us FAKE NEWS.

You can take our official twitter, but you'll never take our free time! #resist

RETWEETS LIKES
9   14

4:31 PM - 25 Jan 2017

Is it because he told them not to talk about climate change? Not entirely, I mean Badlands was one of the first and they do go after him by using scientific facts compared to him. Like the orange mountains that match his skin. Others have stayed true to who they are and only post things related to climate change and how it affects their agency.

With the way that the internet is, it would be hard to completely censor right? Actually no, China for instance is very good at censoring what comes in or goes out of the country. In

2015 during a debate, Trump said that

> "ISIS is recruiting through the internet. ISIS is using the internet better than we are using the internet, and it was our idea. I want to get our brilliant people in Silicon Valley and other places and figure out a way that ISIS cannot do what they're doing. You talk Freedom of Speech. I don't want them to using our internet to take our young, impressionable youth. We should be using our brilliant minds to figure out a way that ISIS cannot use the Internet. And then we should be able to penetrate the Internet and find out exactly where ISIS is and everything about ISIS. And we can do that if we use our good people.

Most of these "good people" he is talking about are foreigners who work for big American tech companies. Which we will discuss the workers later. He doesn't understand how the internet works. It is not a box that you can open and dig through. For us to "stop" ISIS, that would mean we would have to stop social media, stop video sharing, stop forums and message boards. Yes, it would stop anything that allowed one individual to communicate with another.

Does he really believe that the good people we have who rely on that communication not only professionally but personally in our global world would volunteer to close that down? No, but this starts to encroach on the right to free speech. Yes, ISIS is a radical terrorist group. But to effectively shut them down, you would also be shutting down the mom who has a child with a rare birth condition from speaking with other moms around the world who are dealing with the same condition. The internet is a lot more than ISIS and Porn. I mean there are cat videos.

Nationalistic Tendencies

Nationalism can mean many things, to different extents as well. Many will counter by saying that nationalism is just being patriotic to their home country. However, that is being patriotic, which is perfectly acceptable and should be desired by governments around the world. However, that is not being a nationalist. A nationalist, and nationalism are what happens when patriotic feelings are pushed to the extreme. This isn't saying "I want my country to beat all those other countries in the Olympics." That is patriotism.

Nationalism is actually the dark sibling to patriotism, and is a political movement based on self-determination, national solidarity, and not being interfered with by outside influences. This all sounds good, and that all countries should be. However, nationalists push it to the limits of what is needed and what is aggressive. Nationalism isn't new, and many countries have seen varying levels of nationalism within their borders. It is when taken to the extreme that it becomes harmful. There are many different avenues that nationalism can take. Nazi Germany has walked down the path of negative nationalism, and it appears that the United States is starting down a similar route.

Hitler was many things, one being a staunch nationalist. By Hitler aggressively expanding his personal military and calling for a "German Nation" he was practicing what is known as Integral Nationalism, or the desire to create a nation or region that is independent from others. In Nazi Germany, Germans were no longer individuals but as part of a whole. Combine that with statism, the act of a highly-centralized government having control over the economy, at times extending to governmental ownership of industry. This type of nationalism can also break down the ties that bind countries economically. Hitler for example condoned the treaty of Versailles that gave some control of Germany over to other political leaders.

The United States has already seen some indications of these attitudes from Trump. He spoke out against the UN, NATO, and various economic agreements that the US has with other countries. In the first month of his presidency, Trump outwardly spoke out against foreign leaders of allied countries, therefore distancing himself and the United States from political ties. He has already left the Trans-Pacific Partnership which was designed to support economic growth and benefit among the signatories. He is by words and actions ostracizing us from the global community. A community that we need more than it needs us as much as Trump would like to disagree.

One in many conversations of the last month was to consider setting large tariffs against companies and countries that would not work within our borders. Telling both domestic and international companies that if they do not want to build in the United States then they must pay much larger percentages than ever seen, thereby not only hurting companies, but hurting those in the United States that rely on those products. To justify a wall and the move towards nationalism, Sean Spicer, Trumps Press Secretary stated that "a 20% tariff on Mexican imports would raise the necessary funds." Either he doesn't understand how economics works, or they don't care about who buy the imports. When pushed, Trump went to the old standby, Twitter.

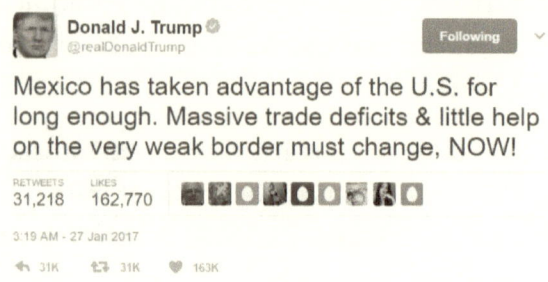

Donald J. Trump @realDonaldTrump

Following

Mexico has taken advantage of the U.S. for long enough. Massive trade deficits & little help on the very weak border must change, NOW!

RETWEETS 31,218   LIKES 162,770

3:19 AM - 27 Jan 2017

31K   31K   163K

Obviously, there is a trade deficit, as the United States has more money than Mexico, and Mexico sells a large percentage of their wares to the United States versus to central/south America.

A tariff on imports will cause the price of the item to rise, thereby causing the consumer to pay more. Since the United States buys 295 billion dollars' worth of goods from Mexico, only third to Canada and China the impact would be substantial. Of that figure 21 billion is agricultural products, such as fruits and vegetables.[42] With many communities suffering from a lack of food security, this could have serious and long term effects on the United States population. Also with the argument that the tariff would result in Mexico paying for the wall, in actuality it is the American consumer that is paying higher prices for everyday items.

Hitler also believed in Ethnic and Religious nationalism. The believe that one ethnic group, the Aryans, were better than anyone else. He also believed that the Jewish as a religion should not be in his version of a nation. These beliefs can at times lead to national purity, which is the case in Nazi Germany. It was Hitler's goal that the German Nation was void of those he did not believe

---

[42] Ivanova, Irina. "What does the U.S. Import from Mexico? A whole lot." CBSNews, January 27, 2017. Found at http://cbsn.ws/2jmwdPK

should exist. His way of ridding the pure of the filth was in the creation of concentration and death camps. His mission, sadly, was highly effective, and millions of Jewish men, women, and children were killed in the name of national purity. Nazi Germany was also a mixture of Territorial Nationalism, and Pan-Nationalism. The belief that not only should all those born inside the boundaries should receive citizenship, but also any Germans that lived outside of the established German boundaries. This became specifically evident when the Alsace Lorraine region between France and Germany was taken back by Germany because of the "German residents."

Not everything went Hitler's way, although most did due to the vast amount of total censorship and the belief that nationalism was paramount to friends, family, or business partners. What Hitler did was calculated, he did not one day wake up and say "All Jews to the ghetto." No, he worked on it slowly and built up the trust of the nation before enacting policy changes. Trump either does not know this, or does not think it applies to him. Trump came from a background where everyone essentially bowed at his feet, and that is not the American way. We fight. We fought Vietnam war, we fought civil rights for African Americans, we fought for Native Americans, and we fought for Homosexual rights. A history book may have helped him before becoming President.

It is not wrong to be civically nationalistic in the belief that everyone born within a specific nation are equal, however it goes too far when everyone is supposed to believe in the same political structure without reserve. Many believe that the United States has a healthy civic nationalism, in that we believe in a republic and voting our leaders in. That is true, however when pushed, it can be justified in punishing those of different political beliefs. While minimally we are beginning to see that in the United States.

Starting with Obama, but really coming to the surface is the hatred and lack of wanting to work with those of different political parties. February 7, 2017 Senator Elizabeth Warren was removed from the senate chambers because she dared to read a letter from Coretta Scott King, the widow of Martin Luther King Jr. Ms. King wrote a scathing letter in 1986 regarding Senator Jeff Sessions when he was looked at for the position of a Federal Judge.[43] Presently he is nominated for the Secretary of State position, and Warren wanted to ensure that those voting were aware of the letter. Republican leaders had Warren removed before she could finish the letter. Whether it was because she was a woman, or because she was adamantly against Sessions, for many of the same reasons as Ms. King, is unknown, but what is known is that later that day, Senator Merkely from Oregon read the letter in the senate chambers without being asked to leave. That is the unintended consequence of civic nationalism being followed to an extreme.

There have been multiple events lately that have shown how nationalistic President Trump and the United States are becoming. The wall between the United States and Mexico was supported under the premise of security. However, it is documented that over 40% of illegal immigrants arrive by plane, and even more come to the United States legally but do not return to their home country when their visa or green cards expire.

The Executive Order not allowing (banning) individuals from war torn Syria and six other countries that are heavily Muslim is also under the guise of national security. There are some real issues with that thought though. The hijackers of the World Trade Center attacks were from Saudi Arabia, United Arab Emirates,

[43] The Coretta Scott King letter Elizabeth Warren was trying to read." CNNPolitics, February 8, 2017. Found at http://cnn.it/2lqukUe

Egypt, and Lebanon. You would expect those countries, at least one of them to be on the "ban" list. The countries that were included were Iraq, Syria, Iran, Sudan, Libya, Somalia, and Yemen. Yes, you read that right, there is so commonality between the two, other than they are predominately Muslim.

Assuming that the President and the administration know the difference between countries, why the disparity? They claim that this was a list that Obama made when he was still President and they were just following along. This is true, but with Obama's list, and administrative action, individuals with valid visas and green cards were not detained. Neither were four-month-old infants needing lifesaving heart surgery. The courts sided with the people that this "ban" was not right and should be at least stayed. Instead of alleviating concerns, or justifying his actions in a mature, and educated manner, the nation gets this argument regarding what it is called. A little back story, even though it is a ban, and they designed it as such, and there are witnesses, they continued to counter with it not being a ban.

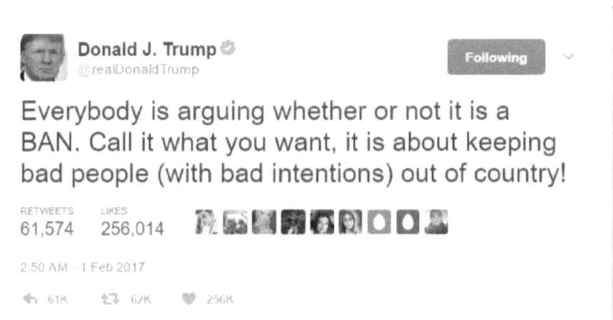

When people did not see it his way, which was kind of expected seeing that many have a civic nationalistic perspective that we are here to help those who need help. Be it four-month-old Islamic babies, or those running from oppression and genocide. This was one tweet in about 40 that had to do with the "ban" and his justification for it.

On February 9, 2017, the Federal district court was finally able to hear arguments from both sides. The court agreed with the people against the federal government that the ban hurt states, businesses, and their tax base. Even though the Federal attorneys attempted to say that the court could not hear it, therefore trying to circumnavigate the intent and purpose of the judicial branch, the courts sides with the states. In now customary fashion the world received this tweet.

Ethical/Security Concerns & Twitter

While not comparable to Hitler as the United States have much different guidelines regarding ethics and how political figures should present themselves, I feel that this is an important subject to briefly discuss. Another element of our current President is the use of Twitter. It has briefly been discussed, but some of it ties in with ethical concerns, and then some is just something that we should all be worried about.

Currently the federal government is full of ethics and national security issues, most of them stemming from Trump and his various business dealings. During the campaign and following the election, Trump had billions of dollars' worth of businesses both domestically and internationally. While having international business dealings is routine, the President has to ensure that none of the businesses have officers from countries that are enemies of the United States. One clear cut way of discovering if there is any ethical conflict of interest issues is to see Trump's tax returns. However, he unequivocally will not release them. He states they are under "audit" but the IRS has stated that it is okay for audited tax returns to be released. The administration had said they will release the statements, but Conway has recently stated that Trump will likely not release them.

On February 10, 2017, Trump flew down to two of his properties with his friends. While going on vacation is not out of the ordinary, the problem arises when they are his properties, and the American taxpayers are funding the trip. Additionally, we do not know the security of the locations, or how much each trip costs. The United States is already paying millions a day for Trump's wife and child to remain in New York at their Trump Tower residence.

Following his weekend trip to Florida, information came to light that there was the possibility of major National Security issues. First, the Florida getaway, Mar-a-Lago, is a Trump owned, private resort that costs $200,000 to become a member. There is no public list of the members, but it is assumed they are wealthy businessmen, and likely some politicians, both American and foreign.

While on this particular trip, North Korea launched a missile in a test fire. Since Trump was entertaining the Japanese Prime Minister, they discussed the matter over dinner. The now former secretary Michael Flynn was also present. This location was not secure, and other guests were within close enough proximity to hear the discussions. In fact those with cell phones could easily capture images of what likely were sensitive documents. If that was not bad enough, fellow guests and wait staff publicly posted on Facebook and Twitter, while the conversation was occurring. This event could have escalated to the point of declaring war, thankfully it did not, but if it had, $200,000 gets you a front row seat apparently.

 Richard DeAgazio added 3 new photos — with Lorin Bertakis and 3 others at 📍 Mar-a-Lago.
Yesterday at 01:35 · Palm Beach, FL · 🌐

HOLY MOLY !!! It was fascinating to watch the flurry of activity at dinner when the news came that North Korea had launched a missile in the direction of Japan. The Prime Minister Abe of Japan huddles with his staff and the President is on the phone with Washington DC. the two world leaders then conferred and then went into another room for hastily arranged press conference. Wow.....the center of the action!!!

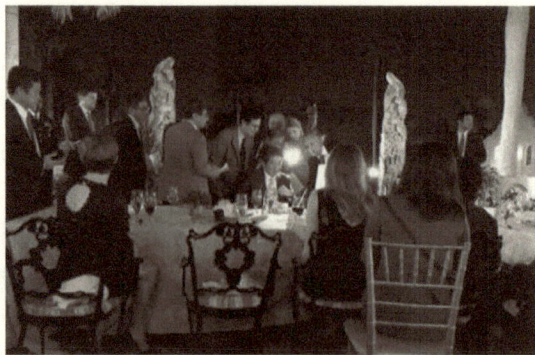

During the same trip, the same guest that posted about the conversations, decided that he not only wanted to meet the individual who carries the "football" — which is a name used for the nuclear briefcase, that is always near the President, and is protected by a military service member — but he wanted to get a selfie with the service member. I blocked out the aide-de-camp's name and the images that he included with this post because, well, honestly it is a national security issue.

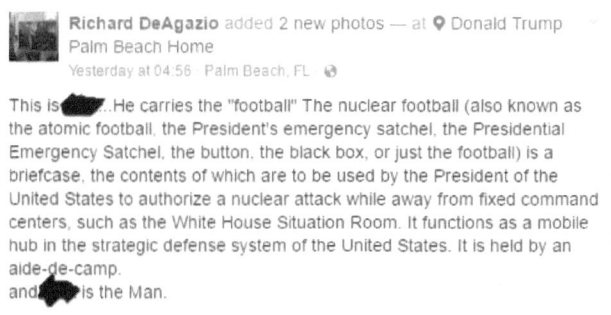

Richard DeAgazio added 2 new photos — at 📍 Donald Trump Palm Beach Home
Yesterday at 04:56 · Palm Beach, FL · 🌐

This is ▓▓.He carries the "football" The nuclear football (also known as the atomic football, the President's emergency satchel, the Presidential Emergency Satchel, the button, the black box, or just the football) is a briefcase, the contents of which are to be used by the President of the United States to authorize a nuclear attack while away from fixed command centers, such as the White House Situation Room. It functions as a mobile hub in the strategic defense system of the United States. It is held by an aide-de-camp.
and ▓▓ is the Man.

While Mar-a-Lago is both an ethics and a national security nightmare, it is not just Trump that are dipping their fingers into the till. Since we are legally bound to protect the Presidential family, that means we are paying the President through his businesses to protect his family. Since we are doing that, why not pay for his son to travel. The American people just paid for his son, Eric to travel to South America to work on a Trump Business deal, to the tune of $100,000.[44] His two sons created a charity in which for 1 million dollars — that will go to an unnamed charity — you could be part of an after inauguration private reception and photo for 16 guests, and either a multi-day hunting or fishing excursion for 4 guests with Donald Trump Jr. and/or Eric Trump,

---

[44]McIntyre, Niamh. "Eric Trump's business trip cost US Taxpayers nearly $100,000 in hotel bills." Independent UK. February 4, 2017. Found at http://ind.pn/2jNCZOU.

in addition to some other smaller mementos. Yes, Trump's sons could have put the newly elected President in mortal danger, to make a buck.[45]

Trump is known for threatening to sue, so is his wife. Daily mail, a British tabloid published an article last year that hinted at the fact that Melania during her modeling career may have been an escort. The man who owned the modeling company denies having an escort business, but he hedges regarding the question exactly, but does admit to owning the model agency that Melania worked for.

In the lawsuit filed by Ms. Trump, she sued, for an obscene amount of money. 150 million to be exact. Why did she sue? Because she states that the article "ruined a unique once-in-a-lifetime opportunity to launch a broad-based commercial brand in multiple product catagories, each of which could have garnered multimillion dollar business relationships for a multiyear [4 years…maybe 8] term during which plaintiff is one of the most photographed women in the world."[46]

Yes, she is saying that because she is first lady, she should be able to make a quick buck. This is technically illegal. While the President, both Trump and Nixon have stated it, cannot actually have conflicts of interest, wives, children, and administration staff can. Do they believe they are so far above the law that conflict of interest does not apply?

---

[45]Levine, Carrie. "Donald Trump's sons behind nonprofit selling access to president-elect." PublicIntegrity, December 19, 2016. Found at http://bit.ly/2hObvvt

[46] Perez-Pena, Richard. "In Libel Suit, Melania Trump cites loss of change to make millions." The New York Times. February 7, 2017. Found at http://nyti.ms/2kEsAHl

Nordstrom recently decided to discontinue Ivanka Trump's clothing and accessories line. They claim that due to an overall decline in sales, they decided to part ways. It happens all the time. Well Trump sees it another way. He believes that it is because she is in the White House with him and it is unfair.

For someone who is a business man it is hard to see how he doesn't understand basic economics. This tweet isn't the problem, since presidents cannot have conflict of interest. However, Presidents cannot do such things as a public employee, which Trump is. One of these things is to do something that specifically assists a family member, close friend, or business partner. Him claiming that Nordstrom was unfair, could cause either Ivanka's brand to be reinstated or picked up by another company. Or the opposite could occur and Nordstrom's may take a hit. It was seen briefly when Trump tweeted about how the US should leave Boeing for Lockheed Martin for the next Air Force One.

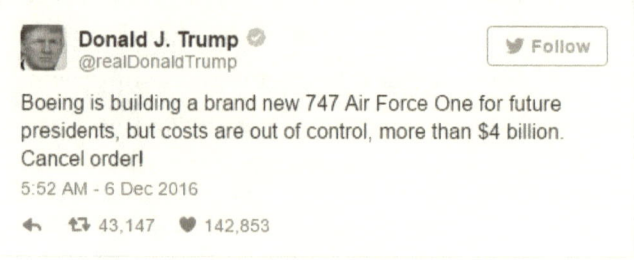

Donald J. Trump @
@realDonaldTrump

Boeing is building a brand new 747 Air Force One for future presidents, but costs are out of control, more than $4 billion. Cancel order!

5:52 AM - 6 Dec 2016

↩ ⟲ 43,147   ♥ 142,853

It was bad enough that Ivanka had her dad try to punish Nordstrom, but what happened February 9, 2017 in the morning really takes the cake. Kellyanne Conway was on Fox news when she was asked about the tweet regarding Ivanka, especially since it was retweeted by the official POTUS Twitter account. She went on about how Ivanka was a wonderful lady, and then said "I think people can see through that. [that Nordstrom removed the line because of her father] Go buy Ivanka's stuff! I hate shopping, and I will go get some today." Okay so she likes the clothing, no big deal right? Well…she continues, "It is just a wonderful line. I own some of it." Still not bad. "I fully, I'm going to give a free commercial here. Go buy it today, everybody. You can find it online."

With that statement Conway broke federal law 5 CFR 2635.702 which states "An employee shall not use or permit the use of its Government position or title or any authority associated with his public office to endorse any product, service, or enterprise."[47] The minute that this was heard, apparently many watchdog groups, including Ethics in Washington, filed complaints with the Office of Government Ethics. The Ethics office claimed they were swamped with calls, faxes, and emails

---

[47] Fang, Marina. "Kellyanne Conway Defends Trump's attack against Nordstrom — By advertising Ivanka's products." February 9, 2017. Found at http://huff.to/2lo0bIv

following the comment. Spicer, in a press conference said "Kellyanne was counseled and that is what we are going to go with." Umm, does that mean they said "Hey Kellyanne, that looks shady, don't do it live anymore." Or will she be punished for breaking a law she should know.

Surely more ethical questions will come up, and it is up to the ethics office along with watchdog groups and the public to ensure the administration is working within the law. There are going to be alternative facts given, but there are people who can, and have been seeing through them. As this book has shown, there are a lot of images from Twitter. Trump enjoys twitter, he uses it frequently, and has stated that he was not going to be giving press conferences because he wanted to interact with the population on social media platforms like Twitter and Facebook. If one wants to stay current, ensure you have either Twitter or Facebook. As President posts should be uplifting, positive, and speaks to the betterment of the nation?

No, it is full of whiny, derogatory, hate-filled rhetoric. Occasionally, you will see niceish posts like the one about his daughter, or when one of his cabinet members is finally confirmed. Most of them however are rants about how the senate isn't moving fast enough, people don't like his "ban", people are talking about him, and fake news. There are some that are truly either intentionally attempting to instigate infighting, or in the case of the Union leader who just said that Trump's numbers were wrong, the cause of death threats. Yes, the President of the United

States tweeted about a private individual to the point that his family's life was in danger.

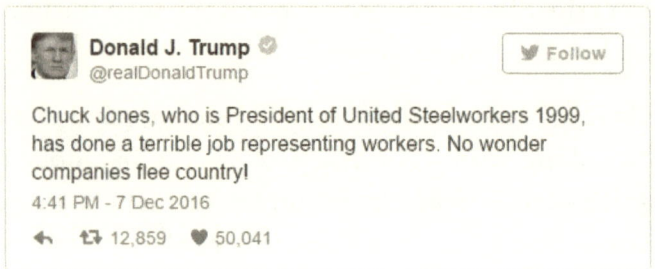

If nothing else, this President will be the most screen shot of probably anyone, dead or alive. He will also likely be the most screen shot for the near future, mostly because no one has taken away his archaic unsecure phone that he uses while his staff works on their private servers when not turning off the required voice recording when Trump talks to Putin, the man he doesn't know.

Conclusion

An important thing to note is that this book is bring written while Trump has been in the White House for less than a month. There will likely be more information and actions that occur after publication. Therefore, this is not an end all be all book. In fact, during the creation of this book, events occurred, and documents signed that affected the narrative. Is it not possible to deliver a book this soon in the presidency that captures all of the likenesses and possible differences.

It does not matter if you voted for Trump, if you voted for Clinton, or if you voted for Johnson or Stein. What matters is an open mind and the ability to admit if you were wrong. If you are someone who voted for Trump and now having second thoughts, see this as an opportunity to fight for what you believe is right, mail your state representatives, send letters, read and think critically. If you did not vote for him, do not cheer that you were right, examine everything still, help to spread the real word, not falsehoods. Before sharing something, make sure it is real.

The one thing that is truly missing is critical thinking, there are too many sheep and not enough herders. That is how the wolf was able to sneak in, no one was watching, no one was concerned until it is too late. Don't be like Germany, don't sit back and let hate rule the day. That is not what the United States was built on, yes we have had our moments, but that doesn't mean we need to do it again. Learn from history and read everything, not just what you like, but read what may scare you, that may upset you, because then you truly know what is going on.

Speak to those who are not your religion, or your ethnicity. You will learn more speaking with someone who is not like you, then you will learn in 100 years of talking to those you are like.

Our world is vast, and beautiful. Take the time to get to know your neighbors, your co-workers, and above all think critically.

Stop rioting, but never stop protesting, rioting makes you and the cause you are for meaningless. One of the reasons the Women's march was so successful was because there were no arrests, the police are not the bad guy, and the marchers knew it. Support those who support you, including those who swore to keep you safe. If you can't support with money or by protesting, sit on the computer and email, help those who can do more.

Is this a book calling Trump a Hitler wannabe? That is for you the reader to decide. Is this a book that shows some common traits? Sure, but that is only as good as the reader decides it is. If nothing else, use this book to see what could happen, see how far down a country can fall before massive and radical changes occur. Even if you think this whole book is rubbish because there are direct, and undeniable comparisons, fine, but that does not mean you should go blindly into the night. Fight for what you believe in because it may be you next who loses a right, and by then there may not be anyone to protest for you.

Do not forget the old saying:

"First they came for the socialists, and I did not speak out — Because I was not a socialist.

Then they came for the trade unionists, and I did not speak out — Because I was not a trade Unionist.

Then they came for the Jews, and I did not speak out — Because I was not a Jew.

Then they came for me — and there was no one left to speak for me."

Don't let that happen, change the rhetoric. The United States is the land of the free because of the brave. We are not free unless we have people who stand up and say "Not here, Not now, Not ever." Be that person, show your children, family, and friends that you will stand up for what is right, that you will be the one saying. "I stand up for you, regardless of who you are, regardless of if I know you, because I hope that you would do the same for me." We all have one life, how do you want to be remembered? Do you want to be that person who let everyone be taken before you and then not have someone stand for you when you are being taken? Or do you want to be that person who stands up and says "Not Today, Not Tomorrow, I stand for and by you."

About the Author

B.M. Williams enjoys spending time exploring the outdoors, really enjoys the rogue badlands twitter feed, and does what any political scientist in this modern day and age does, play on Facebook and read journals. Books are friends, and when it gets bad, and looks dire, pick up a good book, especially a humorous one, and read that. Take a break from your life and immerse yourself in another.

www.ingramcontent.com/pod-product-compliance
Lightning Source LLC
Chambersburg PA
CBHW050358290526
45786CB00003B/1033